KU-471-602

NEW
CHURCH PRAISE

MELODY EDITION

THE SAINT ANDREW PRESS
EDINBURGH

First published 1975
by The Saint Andrew Press
121 George Street Edinburgh
on behalf of
The United Reformed Church in England and Wales
© The United Reformed Church in England and Wales 1975

Reprinted 1979
Reprinted 1980
Reprinted 1983

ISBN 0 7152 0310 X

A Full Music Edition is also available (ISBN 0 7152 0311 8)

Musical art-work by G. E. King
92 Maybury Road, Woking, Surrey

Cover design by J. A. Montgomery

Printed in Great Britain
by Spottiswoode Ballantyne Ltd.
Colchester and London

CONTENTS

		Page
Foreword		v
Preface		vii
Acknowledgements		ix
	Hymn Nos.	
HYMNS (in alphabetical sequence)	1–109	
CANTICLE SETTINGS	110–112	
ORDER OF WORSHIP FOR THE LORD'S SUPPER		127
Alphabetical Index of Tunes		140
Index of Composers, Arrangers & Sources of Tunes		142
Index of Authors, Translators & Sources of Words		144
Index of First Lines		145

FOREWORD

It might have appeared natural that the United Reformed Church should celebrate the achievement of union by producing a new hymn book. The reasons why a Supplement was preferred to a full-size hymn book will be quite clear. In the first place, its production would have taken so long that by the time it appeared the United Reformed Church would be well past the stage of initial celebration. Secondly, a new hymn book was produced for one of our constituent bodies as recently as 1973. Thirdly, it would have been a very expensive business.

But a fourth reason for confining ourselves to a Supplement is more cogent than any of these. It is that at this particular time a Supplement is positively the right kind of book to produce. In this judgment we follow the Methodists, the Baptists, and the Proprietors of Hymns Ancient and Modern who in recent years have brought out Supplements all of which have great distinction and have proved to be exactly what their constituencies needed.

During the past twenty years or so the developments in hymnody, both in words and in music, have been so strenuous and fast-moving that the editors of a full-size hymnal are faced with problems of choice and judgment far more intricate than those which ever faced their predecessors. There is so much new material which appeals to widely differing tastes and interest and which clamours for inclusion that there would be a real danger of a new hymnal's omitting in undue haste much older material simply to make room for the new. Many classics might have been discarded in the zeal to celebrate the contemporary, so that a new generation of hymn singers would be robbed of much that had nourished their fathers. A Supplement, however, means that all that is in the parent book remains available, and that the repertory is simply enriched by a hundred fresh hymns; the only charge for this bonus is the need to provide two hymn books in church instead of one—and in practice other Christian bodies have not found this at all vexatious.

One thing remains to be said. Congregations will enjoy the new book far more, and use it with greater profit, if arrangements can be made for congregational practices, an activity of which some local congregations are still shy. But, with a little planning, it can be done: sometimes briefly within a service at which a new hymn is to be sung; sometimes more extensively on a Sunday or a weekday; and sometimes, very effectively, by congregations gathered in a district or province for a communal introduction to the new material. Such occasions will be all the more valuable if they happen with reasonable regularity.

So we commend *New Church Praise* to the people of the United Reformed Church and to any others who care to use it. It was said in the Preface to *Congregational Praise* that every generation needs its own hymnal. This supplemental book is offered to the present generation in the hope that it will give new vitality and meaning to the parent books which it is designed to augment. May God be pleased to answer the endeavours of the editors in the cheerful, warmhearted and adventurous singing of our congregations.

ERIK ROUTLEY

PREFACE

New Church Praise has been produced in response to a demand within the United Reformed Church for a supplementary collection of hymns which might be used alongside the parent books (*Revised Church Hymnary*, 1927; *The Church Hymnary: Third Edition*, 1973; *Congregational Praise*, 1951) as a vehicle for worship in the last quarter of the twentieth century. The General Assembly of 1973 appointed a special committee to prepare such a hymnbook supplement. This committee had the benefit of the advice of a number of local churches which had taken part, during the previous two years, in a pilot scheme for trying out new material. Many recent hymns have been included, to strengthen the weaker sections of the present books; but earlier centuries have not been ignored—Bunyan, Herbert and Watts may still enrich our prayers and praises. It is hoped that the resulting, varied, collection may therefore be useful as a supplement to other standard hymnbooks besides those used in the United Reformed Church.

Many tunes here presented will be unfamiliar to users of *The Church Hymnary* or *Congregational Praise*, and where suitable alternative tunes may be recommended a cross-reference is provided. A special feature of this book, however, is the frequent interlining of at least the first verse below the melody, in both the full music and the melody editions, and users are encouraged to take advantage of this provision to add many new tunes to their repertoire.

A further feature of this book is the inclusion of an order of worship for the Lord's Supper (Holy Communion), with specially commissioned musical settings of some of the liturgical material. This order was prepared initially for the United Reformed Church by its Doctrine and Worship Committee, but its blend of the traditional and the contemporary may well commend it to Christians of other denominations.

The Committee offers this collection in the hope that it will make some contribution towards the relevance and vitality of the Church's worship for the coming years.

DEO GLORIA

PETER CUTTS (*Chairman*)
DAVID GARDNER (*Secretary*)

ACKNOWLEDGEMENTS

The compilers wish to thank the following who have given permission for copyright material to be printed. Every effort has been made to trace all copyright owners; but if, through inadvertence, any rights have been overlooked, the necessary correction will gladly be made in subsequent editions. Where no entry is shown in the second column, we have been unable to trace (or make contact with) the owner.

MUSIC

COMPOSER OR ARRANGER	OWNER OR CONTROLLER OF COPYRIGHT	HYMN NO.
Ainslie, J.	Composer	82
Alden, J. H.	Composer	38
Bäck, S.		85
Barrett-Ayres, R.	Stainer & Bell Ltd. (from *Songs for the Seventies*)	2, 8(ii)
Bartlett, L. F.	Composer	80(i)
Blake, L.	Composer	39, 43
Brent Smith A.		15(ii)
Carter, S..	Stainer & Bell Ltd. (from *Songs of Sydney Carter in the Present Tense*)	20
,,	Stainer & Bell Ltd.	41
Cutts, P.	Oxford University Press	1(i), 4, 24(ii), 40, 48(i), 52, 54, 55, 74, 91, 97, 101, 108
Darke, H.	Proprietors of *Hymns Ancient and Modern*	76
Dearnley, C.	Composer	75
Dykes Bower, J.	Proprietors of *Hymns Ancient and Modern*	14
Dyson, G.	Novello and Company Ltd.	92
Evans, D.	Oxford University Press (from *Revised Church Hymnary*) 10 harm., 18 harm.	
Gardner, J.	Composer	28
Goodall, D.	British Weekly Ltd.	42
,,	Composer	107
Gooding, Y.	National Christian Education Council 1973	90
Green, J.	Vanguard Music Ltd., 12 Portland Road, London S.E. 25	50
Harris, W. H.	The Executrix for the late Sir William Harris	46, 63
Holst, G.	Roberton Publications (for J. Curwen & Sons Ltd.).	30 (arr.)
Hutchings, A. J. B.	Oxford University Press (from *English Hymnal Service Book*)	17
Jacquet, R. H.	Composer	83, 88
Jagger, A. T. I.	United Reformed Church in England and Wales	19
Langlais, J.	Société des editions Philippo, Paris	36
Laycock, G.	Faber Music Ltd., London (from *New Catholic Hymnal*)	71, 84 (arr.)
Llewellyn, W.	Oxford University Press	86
Loring, J. H..	Composer	69
McCarthy, D.	Composer	87
Micklem, T. C.	Composer	3, 6, 8(i), 16, 22, 27, 32, 48(ii), 61, 68, 73, 93(i), 102, 104
Moe, D.	Augsburg Publishing House.	58
Murray, A. G.	Composer	29
Newport, D.	Composer	62
Potter, D.	Composer	9
Reid, E.	Stainer & Bell Ltd. (from *New Songs of the Church Book 1*)	23, 100
,,	H. C. Reid	31

Routley, E.	from *Eternal Light* (Carl Fischer Inc. Cat. No. 0 4877) © MCMLXXI by Carl Fischer, Inc. New York. International Copyright secured. All rights reserved . . . 7, 24(i), 94
„	Stainer & Bell Ltd. (from *New Songs for the Church Book 1*) . 21
„	Composer 33, 53, 56, 57, 110, 111, 112,
Schweizer, R.	© 1966 Hänssler-Verlag, Neuhausen-Stuttgart (from *Bausteine für den Gottesdienst*) 89
Sharpe, E.	Oxford University Press (from *Enlarged Songs of Praise*) . . 5
Shaw, M.	Oxford University Press (from *Enlarged Songs of Praise*) 72 harm.
„	Oxford University Press (from *Oxford Book of Carols*) 81 harm.
Sheldon, R.	Composer . . . . 51 (with descant)
Stanton, W. K. . . .	Oxford University Press (from *B.B.C. Hymn Book*) . . . 37
Stocks, G. G.	The Governors of Repton School 13
Strange, C. E.	Composer . . . . 93(ii)
Thiman, E. H.	Composer . . . . 80(ii) harm.
Westbrook, F.	The Methodist Church: Division of Education and Youth . 47
Williams, D.	Composer 60
Williams, R. Vaughan .	Oxford University Press (from *English Hymnal*) . . . 34 arr.
„	Oxford University Press (from *Enlarged Songs of Praise*) . 77 arr.
Williams, R. Vaughan (har.) and Broadwood, L. (mel.)	Oxford University Press (from *English Hymnal*) . . . 95
Wilson, J.	Composer . . . . 65, 80(i) descants
„	Oxford University Press 98
Wren, B. A.	Oxford University Press 99
Young, C. R.	Harmonisation © 1965: Abingdon Press . . . . . 1(ii)
Zimmermann, H. W. . .	From *Five Hymns* by Heinz Werner Zimmermann, copyright 1973 by Concordia Publishing House. Used by permission 79

WORDS

AUTHOR OR TRANSLATOR	OWNER OR CONTROLLER OF COPYRIGHT	HYMN NO.
Appleford, P.	Josef Weinberger Ltd., from *27 20th Century Hymns* . .	46
Arlott, J.	Author	34
Bayly, A. F.	Author . . . . 48, 60 (part), 78, 109	
Bonhoeffer, D.	S.C.M. Press ('Christians and Pagans' in *Letters and Papers from Prison* rev. ed. 1967 Versified by W. H. Farquharson)	63
Bridge, B. E.	Free Church Choir Union	96
Bridges, R.	Oxford University Press (from *The Yattendon Hymnal*) .	64
Burkitt, F. C.	Society for Promoting Christian Knowledge	76
Caird, G. B.	Author	67
Carter, S.	Stainer & Bell Ltd. (from *Songs of Sydney Carter in the Present Tense*)	20
„	Stainer & Bell Ltd.	41
Collihole, M.	Stainer & Bell Ltd. (from *New Orbit*)	83
Cropper, M.	. . . . 45, 95	
Dearmer, P.	Oxford University Press (from *Songs of Praise*) . . .	30
„	Oxford University Press (from *Oxford Book of Carols*) .	72, 81
Dudley-Smith, T. . . .	Author	92
Dunn, V.	Vanguard Music Ltd., 12, Portland Road, London S.E.25 .	50
Ferguson, J.	Stainer & Bell Ltd. (from *Songs for the Seventies*) . . .	2
Fraser, I.	Stainer & Bell Ltd. (from *Songs for the Seventies*) . . .	8
„	Stainer & Bell Ltd. (from *New Songs for the Church Book 1*) .	54
Gaunt, A.	John Paul: The Preacher's Press	13, 56
Gaunt, H. C. A. . . .	Author	14, 73
Geyer, J. B.	Stainer & Bell Ltd. (from *New Songs for the Church Book 1*) .	23
Gill, D. M.	Author	12

Goodall, D.	British Weekly Ltd.	42
,,	Author	108
Green, F. Pratt	Oxford University Press	10, 28, 51, 59, 87, 94, 106
,,	© Hänssler-Verlag, Neuhausen-Stuttgart (from *Cantate Domino*, English text)	89
Gregory, J. K.	Author	19, 107
,,	Proprietors of *Hymns Ancient and Modern*	37
Hartman, O.		85
Herklots, R. E.	Oxford University Press	25
Herve, M. O.	Mayhew-McCrimmon Ltd.	88
Hewlett, M.	Stainer & Bell Ltd. (from *Contemporary loose leaf Hymn Book*)	75
Hilton, D.	National Christian Education Council. 1973	90
Hughes, D. W.	Mr. J. R. Hughes.	7, 17
Icarus P.	Mayhew-McCrimmon Ltd.	82, 97
Jillson, M.	Author	79
Johnson, R.	Author	36; refrain
Jones, R. G.	Author	32
Kaan, F.	Stainer & Bell Ltd. (from *Songs for the Seventies*)	5, 33, 53
,,	Stainer & Bell Ltd. (from *Pilgrim Praise*)	70, 71, 77, 80, 91
,,	Reproduced by permission of B. Feldman & Co., Ltd. 138–140, Charing Cross Road, London W.C.2.	103
King, G.	Stainer & Bell Ltd. (from *New Orbit*)	105
Luff, A.	Stainer & Bell Ltd. (from *New Songs for the Church Book 2*)	21
Micklem, R. and T. C.	Authors	85
Micklem, T. C.	Author	3, 16, 22, 27, 69, 101, 104
,,	H. Freeman & Co. 137/140 Charing Cross Road, London W.C.2.	6
New English Bible	*New English Bible* 2nd edition 1970 by permission of Oxford and Cambridge Univ. Presses	68
North Ghana	The Iona Community	44
O'Neill, J.	Author	62
Orchard, S.	Author	61
Phillips, N.	United Reformed Church in England and Wales	43
Pilcher, C. V.	F. E. V. Pilcher	35
Quinn, J.	Geoffrey Chapman Publishers	29
Reid, E.	H. C. Reid	31
,,	Stainer & Bell Ltd. (from *New Songs for the Church Book 1*)	100
Rimaud, D.		36
Routley, E.	Stainer & Bell Ltd. (from *New Songs for the Church Book 1*)	1
,,	Author	66
Thompson, C.	Author	11
Wren, B. A.	Oxford University Press	9, 18, 36 (part), 39, 40, 52, 55, 57, 58, 74, 93, 98, 99, 102
,,	S.C.M. Press (from *Contemporary Prayers for Public Worship* 1967)	24

We are also grateful to Dame Helen Gardner for her gloss on the words of Hymn No. 15.

1

BIRABUS

Peter Cutts (b. 1937)

All who love and serve your ci - ty, all who bear its dai-ly stress,

all who cry for peace and jus - tice, all who curse and all who bless,

SECOND TUNE

CHARLESTOWN

Stephen Jenks's *American Compiler of Sacred Harmony, No. 1*, 1803.
Harmonised by Carlton R. Young (b. 1926)

All who love and serve your ci - ty, all who bear its dai - ly stress,

all who cry for peace and justice, all who curse and all who bless,

'The Lord is there'

1 All who love and serve your city,
    all who bear its daily stress,
  all who cry for peace and justice,
    all who curse and all who bless,

2 in your day of loss and sorrow,
    in your day of helpless strife,
  honour, peace and love retreating,
    seek the Lord, who is your life.

3 In your day of wealth and plenty,
    wasted work and wasted play,
  call to mind the word of Jesus,
    'Work ye yet while it is day'.

4 For all days are days of judgment,
    and the Lord is waiting still,
  drawing near to men who spurn him,
    offering peace from Calvary's hill.

5 Risen Lord! shall yet the city
    be the city of despair?
  Come today, our Judge, our Glory;
    be its name, 'The Lord is there!'

Erik Routley (b. 1917)

2

ABEL

REGINALD BARRETT-AYRES (b. 1920)

'Am I my bro-ther's keep-er?'—the mut-tered cry was drowned by A-bel's lifeblood shouting in si-lence from the ground. For no man is an is-land di-vi-ded from the main, the bell which tolled for A-bel tolled e-qual-ly for Cain.

CODA (after V.3)

My brother's keeper

1 'Am I my brother's keeper?'—
   the muttered cry was drowned
   by Abel's life-blood shouting
   in silence from the ground.
   For no man is an island
   divided from the main,
   the bell which tolled for Abel
   tolled equally for Cain.

2 The ruler called for water
   and thought his hands were clean.
   Christ counted less than order,
   the man than the machine.
   The crowd cried, 'Crucify him!',
   their malice wouldn't budge,
   so Pilate called for water,
   and history's his judge.

3 As long as people hunger,
   as long as people thirst,
   and ignorance and illness
   and warfare do their worst,
   as long as there's injustice
   in any of God's lands,
   I am my brother's keeper,
   I dare not wash my hands.

John Ferguson (b. 1921)

3
LUMIS

Caryl Micklem (b. 1925)

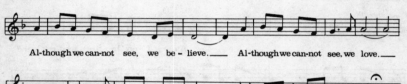

Al-though we can-not see, we be - lieve.___ Al-though we can-not see, we love.___

Un-known God, be known to us in Christ, and in our shar-ing of the search.

Caryl Micklem (b. 1925)

This single-verse hymn is meant to be sung (by choir or congregation) as a response to spoken prayer or reading, perhaps repeated several times in the course of a service or of one act of prayer within it. See also 68, 69.

4

BRIDEGROOM

PETER CUTTS (b. 1937)

As the bride-groom to his cho — sen, as the king un-to his realm,

as the keep un — to the cas — tle, as the pi-lot to the helm,

so, _____ Lord, art thou _____ to me.

A and B may be sung by contrasted groups of voices.

Belonging

1 As the bridegroom to his chosen,
    as the king unto his realm,
    as the keep unto the castle,
    as the pilot to the helm,
      so, Lord, art thou to me.

2 As the fountain in the garden,
    as the candle in the dark,
    as the treasure in the coffer,
    as the manna in the ark,
      so, Lord, art thou to me.

3 As the music at the banquet,
    as the stamp unto the seal,
    as the medicine to the fainting,
    as the wine-cup at the meal,
      so, Lord, art thou to me.

4 As the ruby in the setting,
    as the honey in the comb,
    as the light within the lantern,
    as the father in the home,
      so, Lord, art thou to me.

5 As the sunshine in the heavens,
    as the image in the glass,
    as the fruit unto the fig-tree,
    as the dew unto the grass,
      so, Lord, art thou to me.

Par. from John Tauler (1300–61)
by Emma Frances Bevan (1827–1909)

5

PLATTS LANE

EVELYN SHARPE (1884–1969)
and compilers

As we break the bread and taste the life of wine,

we bring to mind our Lord, man of all time.

1 As we break the bread
    and taste the life of wine,
  we bring to mind our Lord,
    man of all time.

2 Grain is sown to die;
    it rises from the dead,
  becomes through human toil
    our common bread.

3 Pass from hand to hand
    the living love of Christ!
  Machine and man provide
    bread for this feast.

4 Jesus binds in one
    our daily life and work;
  he is of all mankind
    symbol and mark.

5 Having shared the bread
    that died to rise again,
  we rise to serve the world,
    scattered as grain.

Fred Kaan (b. 1929)

6

PADDOCK PLACE

CARYL MICKLEM (b. 1925)
and compilers

A-wake from sleep, the night is spent! The morn-ing star moves up the sky: the hosts of heav'n, with sweet con-sent, pro-claim sal – va-tion's time is high. Come, praise the long — im-plored, our Sa-viour, Christ the Lord!

The House of Bread

1 Awake from sleep, the night is spent!
   The morning star moves up the sky:
the hosts of heaven, with sweet consent,
   proclaim salvation's time is high.
      Come, praise the long-implored,
      our Saviour, Christ the Lord!

2 While man, the rather sin to choose,
   prepares the purple, plants the thorn,
the Word of God our flesh endues
   that we, by will of God reborn,
      the sons of God may be
      to all eternity.

3 Let regal power and humble beast
   and shepherd, serving both, attend;
since all, from greatest unto least,
   are proffered bliss which shall not
                              [end,
      where spreads his banquet-board
      our Saviour, Christ the Lord.

4 In Bethlehem, the House of Bread,
   a richer harvest now is sown;
for none at Jesus' table fed
   shall ever thirst or hunger own,
      but shall from foes be free
      to all eternity.

5 Greet the fulfilment of your dreams,
   sad earth, by Adam's plague oppressed!
May he whose lowliness redeems
   both north and south, both east and west,
      now be by all adored,
      our Saviour, Christ the Lord.

Caryl Micklem (b. 1925)

(v. 4) 'Beth-lehem' means in Hebrew 'house of bread'.

7

MAIDEN WAY

ERIK ROUTLEY (b. 1917)

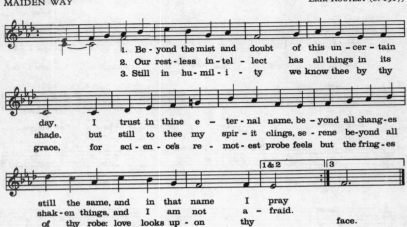

1. Be - yond the mist and doubt of this un - cer - tain
2. Our rest - less in - tel - lect has all things in its
3. Still in hu - mil - i - ty we know thee by thy

day, I trust in thine e - ter - nal name, be - yond all chang - es
shade, but still to thee my spir - it clings, se - rene be - yond all
grace, for sci - en - ce's re - mot - est probe feels but the fring - es

still the same, and in that name I pray
shak - en things, and I am not a - fraid.
of thy robe: love looks up - on thy face.

Credo

1　Beyond the mist and doubt
　　of this uncertain day,
　　I trust in thine eternal name,
　　beyond all changes still the same,
　　and in that name I pray.

2　Our restless intellect
　　has all things in its shade,
　　but still to thee my spirit clings,
　　serene beyond all shaken things,
　　and I am not afraid.

3　Still in humility
　　we know thee by thy grace,
　　for science's remotest probe
　　feels but the fringes of thy robe:
　　love looks upon thy face.

Donald Hughes (1911–67)

8

FIRST TUNE

RODEL

CARYL MICKLEM (b. 1925)

(Verses 3 – 4)

CHRIST, burn - ing past all suns, stars be - neath thy feet like leaves on fo - rest floor:

MAN, turning spaceward, shuns knowledge in - com - plete, fe - vered to ex - plore ___

SECOND TUNE

REGINALD BARRETT-AYRES (b. 1920)
arranged by compilers

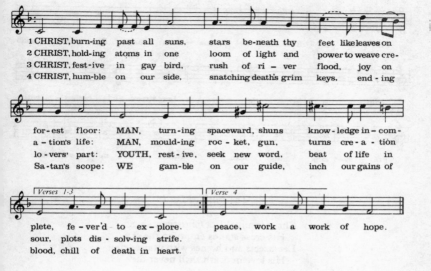

1 CHRIST, burning past all suns,
    stars beneath thy feet like leaves on forest floor:
MAN, turning spaceward, shuns
    knowledge incomplete, fevered to explore.

2 CHRIST, holding atoms in one
    loom of light and power to weave creation's life:
MAN, moulding rocket, gun,
    turns creation sour, plots dissolving strife.

3 CHRIST, festive in gay bird,
    rush of river flood, joy on lovers' part:
YOUTH, restive, seek new word,
    beat of life in blood, chill of death in heart.

4 CHRIST, humble on our side,
    snatching death's grim keys, ending Satan's scope:
WE gamble on our guide,
    inch our gains of peace, work a work of hope.

Ian Fraser (b. 1917)

The antitheses may be brought out by dividing each verse except the last between two bodies of singers.

9

DOREEN POTTER in *Cantate Domino*, 1974

Christ is a - live!___ Let Chris - tians sing. His cross stands

emp - ty to the sky. Let streets and homes___ with

prai - ses ring. His love in death___ shall ne - ver die.

The crucified Lord

1 Christ is alive! Let Christians sing.
   His cross stands empty to the sky.
   Let streets and homes with praises ring.
   His love in death shall never die.

2 Christ is alive! No longer bound
      to distant years in Palestine
   he comes to claim the here and now
      and conquer every place and time.

3 Not throned above, remotely high,
      untouched, unmoved by human pains
   but daily, in the midst of life,
      our Saviour with the Father reigns.

4 In every insult, rift and war
      where colour, scorn or wealth divide
   he suffers still, yet loves the more,
      and lives, though ever crucified.

5 Christ is alive! Ascendant Lord,
      he rules the world his Father made
   till, in the end, his love adored
      shall be to every man displayed.

Brian Wren (b. 1936)

10
CHRISTE SANCTORUM

Melody from *Paris Antiphoner*, 1681
harmonised by DAVID EVANS (1874–1948)

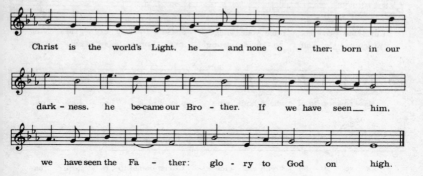

Christ is the world's Light, he ___ and none o - ther; born in our dark - ness, he be-came our Bro - ther. If we have seen ___ him, we have seen the Fa - ther: glo - ry to God on high.

The uniqueness of Christ

1 Christ is the world's Light, he and none other;
born in our darkness, he became our Brother.
If we have seen him, we have seen the Father:
glory to God on high.

2 Christ is the world's Peace, he and none other;
no man can serve him and despise his brother.
Who else unites us, one in God the Father?
glory to God on high.

3 Christ is the world's Life, he and none other;
sold once for silver, murdered here, our Brother—
he, who redeems us, reigns with God the Father:
glory to God on high.

4 Give God the glory, God and none other;
give God the glory, Spirit, Son and Father;
give God the glory, God in man my brother;
glory to God on high.

F. Pratt Green (b. 1903)

11

AVE, VIRGO VIRGINUM

Melody from Horn's *Gesangbuch*, 1544

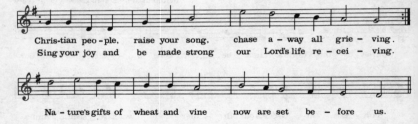

Chris-tian peo-ple, raise your song. chase a-way all grie-ving.
Sing your joy and be made strong our Lord's life re-cei-ving.

Na-ture's gifts of wheat and vine now are set be-fore us.

as we of-fer bread and wine Christ comes to re-store us.

At the offering of bread and wine

1 Christian people, raise your song,
    chase away all grieving.
  Sing your joy and be made strong
    our Lord's life receiving.
  Nature's gifts of wheat and vine
    now are set before us:
  as we offer bread and wine
    Christ comes to restore us.

2 Come to welcome Christ today,
    God's great revelation.
  He has pioneered the way
    of the new creation.
  Greet him, Christ our risen king
    gladly recognizing,
  as with joy men greet the spring
    out of winter rising.

Colin P. Thompson (b. 1945)

12

POLZEATH

English Traditional Carol Melody
arranged by compilers

Come let us re — mem - ber the joys of the town:

gay vans and bright bus – es that roar up and down,

shop - win - dows and playgrounds and swings in the park,

and street - lamps that twin - kle in rows af - ter dark.

1 Come, let us remember the joys of the town:
  gay vans and bright buses that roar up and down,
  shop-windows and playgrounds and swings in the park,
  and street-lamps that twinkle in rows after dark.

2 And let us remember the chorus that swells
  from hooters and hammers and whistles and bells,
  from fierce-panting engines and clear-striking clocks,
  and sirens of vessels afloat in the docks.

3 Come, let us now lift up our voices in praise,
  and to the Creator a thanksgiving raise,
  for towns with their buildings of stone, steel and wood,
  for people who love them and work for their good.

4 We thank thee, O God, for the numberless things
  and friends and adventures which every day brings.
  O may we not rest until all that we see
  in towns and in cities is pleasing to thee.

Doris M. Gill
(One verse omitted)

13

SUNSET

G. G. STOCKS (1877–1960)

Come, liv-ing God, when least ex-pec-ted, when minds are dull and hearts are cold,

thro' sharp'ning word and warm af-fec-tion, re-veal-ing truths as yet un-told.

1 Come, living God, when least expected,
　　when minds are dull and hearts are cold,
　through sharpening word and warm affection
　　revealing truths as yet untold.

2 Break from the tomb in which we hide you
　　to speak again in startling ways;
　break through the words in which we bind you
　　to resurrect our lifeless praise.

3 Come now, as once you came to Moses
　　within the bush alive with flame,
　or to Elijah on the mountain,
　　by silence pressing home your claim.

4 So, let our minds be sharp to read you
　　in sight or sound or printed page,
　and let us greet you in our neighbours,
　　in flaming youth or quiet age.

5 Then, from our gloom, your Son still rising
　　will thaw the frozen heart of pride
　and flash upon us through the shadows
　　to spread his resurrection wide.

6 And we will share his radiant brightness
　　and, blazing through the dread of night,
　illuminate by love and reason,
　　for men in darkness, faith's delight.

Alan Gaunt (b. 1935)

14

JOHN DYKES BOWER (b. 1905)

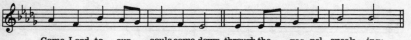

Come, Lord, to our— souls come down, through the— gos-pel speak-ing;

let your words, your cross and crown, light-en all our— seek-ing.

The gospel

1 Come, Lord, to our souls come down,
    through the gospel speaking;
  let your words, your cross and crown,
    lighten all our seeking.

2 Drive out darkness from the heart,
    banish pride and blindness;
  plant in every inward part
    truthfulness and kindness.

3 Eyes be open, spirits stirred,
    minds new truth receiving;
  make us, Lord, by your own Word,
    more and more believing.

H. C. A. Gaunt (b. 1902)

15

FIRST TUNE

TUNBRIDGE

Melody by JEREMIAH CLARKE (c. 1673–1707)

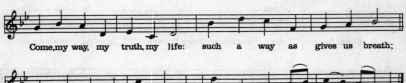

Come, my way, my truth, my life: such a way as gives us breath;

such a truth as ends all strife; such a life as kill - eth death.

SECOND TUNE

COME MY WAY

A. BRENT SMITH (1899–1950)

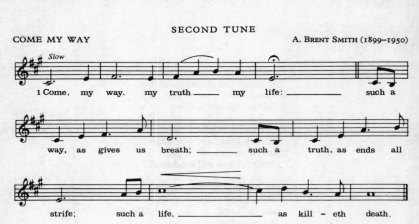

1 Come, my way, my truth, my life: such a way, as gives us breath; such a truth, as ends all strife; such a life, as kill - eth death.

The call

1 Come, my way, my truth, my life:
    such a way as gives us breath;
    such a truth as ends all strife;
    such a life as killeth death.

2 Come, my light, my feast, my strength:
    such a light as shows a feast;
    such a feast as mends in length;
    such a strength as makes his guest.

3 Come, my joy, my love, my heart:
    such a joy as none can move;
    such a love as none can part;
    such a heart as joys in love.

George Herbert (1593–1633)

(v. 2) 'mends in length' means 'grows better as it goes on': cf. *John* 2.10.

16

DOLLIS BROOK

CARYL MICKLEM (b. 1925)

1. Come to our homes to stay, Lord of this wedd-ing day: come to us
2. Fa-ther of all, to you prai-ses and thanks are due: fam-il-ies

from a-bove to break the bread of love. Ev-ery good gift that
ev-ery-where re-flect your lov-ing care. Make of our lives to-

hal-lows our hu-man life your mind con-ceived and shaped. You and your
geth-er a ho-ly thing, hea-ven on earth be-low, so that to

Church are close as man and wife or pro-mise made and kept.
all who meet our love we bring Christ as the Lord we know.

At a wedding

1   Come to our homes to stay,
         Lord of this wedding day:
         come to us from above
         to break the bread of love.
Every good gift that hallows our human life
    your mind conceived and shaped.
You and your Church are close as man and wife
    or promise made and kept.

2   Father of all, to you
         praises and thanks are due:
         families everywhere
         reflect your loving care.
Make of our lives together a holy thing,
    heaven on earth below,
so that to all who meet our love we bring
    Christ as the Lord we know.

Caryl Micklem (b. 1925)

17

FUDGIE

ARTHUR J. B. HUTCHINGS (b. 1906)

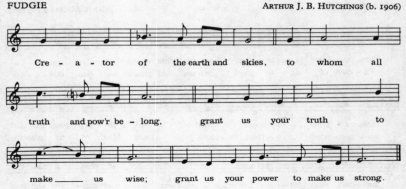

Cre - a - tor of the earth and skies, to whom all truth and pow'r be - long, grant us your truth to make _____ us wise; grant us your power to make us strong.

Penitence

1 Creator of the earth and skies,
    to whom all truth and power belong,
  grant us your truth to make us wise;
    grant us your power to make us strong.

2 We have not known you: to the skies
    our monuments of folly soar,
  and all our self-wrought miseries
    have made us trust ourselves the more.

3 We have not loved you: far and wide
    the wreckage of our hatred spreads,
  and evils wrought by human pride
    recoil on unrepentant heads.

4 We long to end this worldwide strife:
    how shall we follow in your way?
  Speak to mankind your words of life,
    until our darkness turns to day.

Donald Hughes (1911–67), *altd.*

18

DURROW

Irish traditional melody set by DAVID EVANS (1874–1948)

Deep in the shadows of the past, far out from set-tled lands,

some no-mads travelled with their God a – cross the de-sert sands.

The dawn of hope for all mankind was glimpsed by them a - lone

a promise call-ing them ahead, a fu-ture yet un – known.

The quest

1 Deep in the shadows of the past,
    far out from settled lands,
  some nomads travelled with their God
    across the desert sands.
  The dawn of hope for all mankind
    was glimpsed by them alone—
  a promise calling them ahead,
    a future yet unknown.

2 While others bowed to changeless gods
    they met a mystery:
  God with an uncompleted name,
    'I am what I will be';
  and by their tents, around their fires,
    in story, song and law
  they praised, remembered, handed on
    a past that promised more.

3 From Abraham to Nazareth
    the promise changed and grew
  while some, remembering the past,
    recorded what they knew,
  and some, in letters or laments,
    in prophecy and praise,
  recovered, held and re-expressed
    new hope for changing days.

4 For all the writings that survived,
    for leaders, long ago,
  who sifted, chose, and then preserved
    the Bible that we know,
  give thanks, and find its promise yet
    our comfort, strength and call—
  the working model for our faith
    alive with hope for all.

Brian Wren (b. 1936)

(v. 2) with lines 3 and 4 cf. *Exodus* 3.13 NEB and margin.

19

Ear - ly morn - ing. 'Come pre - pare him, to the tomb your spi - ces bring; death is cold and death de - cay - ing, we must beau - ti - fy our king.'

Easter morning

1 Early morning. 'Come, prepare him,
    to the tomb your spices bring;
  death is cold and death decaying,
    we must beautify our king.'

2 Early morning, women excited,
    seeking Peter everywhere;
  telling of a man who told them,
    'He is risen. Don't despair'.

3 Peter racing, early morning,
    to the tomb and rushing in;
  seeing shrouds of death dispensed with,
    finding new-born faith begin.

4 Early morning, Mary weeping,
    asking if the gardener knew;
  knowing, as his voice says, 'Mary',
    'Lord, Rabbuni, it is you'.

5 'Mary, you can live without me,
    as I now to God ascend;
  peace be with you; I am with you
    early morning without end.'

6 Early morning, stay for ever,
    early morning, never cease;
  early morning, come to all men
    for their good and power and peace.

John Gregory (b. 1929)

20

SYDNEY CARTER (b. 1915)

1. Ev – ery star shall sing a car-ol; ev – ery crea-ture, high or low,

come and praise the king of hea-ven by what-ev – er name you know:

REFRAIN

God a – bove, man be – low, ho – ly, is the name I know.

A carol of the universe

1 Every star shall sing a carol;
    every creature, high or low,
  come and praise the king of heaven
    by whatever name you know.
  God above, man below,
    holy is the name I know.

2 When the king of all creation
    had a cradle on the earth,
  holy was the human body,
    holy was the human birth.

3 Who can tell what other cradle,
    high above the Milky Way,
  still may rock the king of heaven
    on another Christmas day?

4 Who can count how many crosses,
    still to come or long ago,
  crucify the king of heaven?
    Holy is the name I know.

5 Who can tell what other body
    he will hallow for his own?
  I will praise the son of Mary,
    brother of my blood and bone.

6 Every star and every planet,
    every creature, high and low,
  come and praise the king of heaven
    by whatever name you know.

Sydney Carter (b. 1915)

ANTIPHON 1 (*Sung by the* Choir)
allegro (○=○ *of Verses*)

TE DEUM
('You we praise as God')

ERIK ROUTLEY (b. 1917)

Ex - tol the Lord your God, for the Lord your God is ho - ly.

Verses 1-5
People in unison

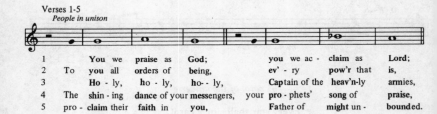

1		You we	praise as	God;	you we ac -	claim as	Lord;
2	To	you all	orders of	being,	ev' - ry	pow'r that	is,
3		Ho - ly,	ho - ly,	ho-- ly,	Captain of the	heav'n-ly	armies,
4	The	shin - ing	dance of your	messengers,	your pro - phets'	song of	praise,
5		pro - claim their	faith in	you,	Father of	might un -	bounded.

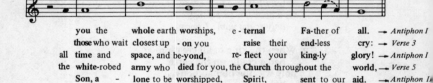

you the	whole earth worships,	e - ternal	Fa-ther of	all.	→ *Antiphon I*
those who wait	closest up - on you	raise their	end-less	cry:	→ *Verse 3*
all time and	space, and be-yond,	re- flect your	king-ly	glory!	→ *Antiphon I*
the white-robed	army who died for you, the	Church throughout the		world,	→ *Verse 5*
Son, a -	lone to be worshipped,	Spirit,		sent to our aid.	→ *Antiphon I*

ANTIPHON II *(Sung by the* Choir)

(○=○ of Verses)

Solo *(or a few voices)*　　　　　　　　　　Chorus

Who is the king of glo - ry?___ The Lord of hosts, he is the king of glory!

Verses 6-8
People in unison

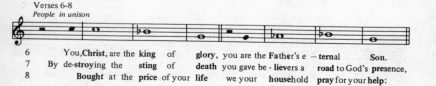

6　　　You, Christ, are the **king** of　　**glory,** you are the Father's e – **ternal**　　　**Son.**
7　　By de-**stroying** the **sting** of　　**death** you gave be - lievers a　　**road** to God's **presence,**
8　　　　**Bought** at the **price** of your **life**　　we your　　**household** **pray** for your **help:**

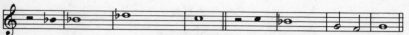

When to **save** the **world** you became **man,**　you did not **shrink** from a **hu-**man　**birth.** →
　　　Antiphon II
where you **sit** en-**throned** in　　　　**light;** we a – **wait** your **coming** as **Judge.** →
　　　Verse 8
　　　　give us the **fulness** of　　**life**　　for　　ever with　**all** who are **yours.** →
　　　Antiphon II

AFTER THE LAST ANTIPHON – TO BE SUNG BY ALL:

(○ = ○ of verses)

AL – LE – LU — IA,　　　AL – LE – LU — IA!

Latin, c. 400.　Tr. Alan Luff. (b. 1928)

22
ALL KINDS OF LIGHT

CARYL MICKLEM (b. 1925)

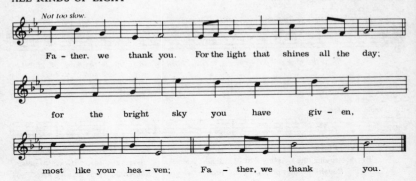

Fa-ther, we thank you. For the light that shines all the day; for the bright sky you have giv-en, most like your hea-ven; Fa-ther, we thank you.

All kinds of light

1 Father, we thank you.
For the light that shines all the day;
for the bright sky you have given,
most like your heaven;
Father, we thank you.

2 Father, we thank you.
For the lamps that lighten the way;
for human skill's exploration
of your creation;
Father, we thank you.

3 Father, we thank you.
For the friends who brighten our play;
for your command to call others
sisters and brothers;
Father, we thank you.

4 Father, we thank you.
For your love in Jesus today,
giving us hope for tomorrow
through joy and sorrow;
Father, we thank you.

Caryl Micklem (b. 1925)

23

WESTHOLME   ERIC REID (1936–1970)

Fire is light-ing torch and lamp at night, fire out-bursts in-to power and light. Come, O God, Cre - a - tor, Spi - rit, now, fill all our lives with your fire. [Vv 1 & 2] [V.3] light.

Creator Spirit

1 Fire is lighting torch and lamp at night,
   fire outbursts into power and light.
      Come, O God, Creator, Spirit, now,
      fill all our lives with your fire.

2 Wind is battering waves of sea on land;
   wind is grinding the rocks to sand.
      Come, O God, Creator, Spirit, now,
      fill all the world with your power.

3 Water gushes down the cleft of space,
   living water and spring of grace.
      Come, O God, Creator, Spirit, now,
      grant us your life and your light.

John B. Geyer (b. 1932), *altd.*

FIRST TUNE

THE HAYES

ERIK ROUTLEY (b. 1917)

Solo or Semichorus

For the bread that we have ea - ten, for the wine that we have

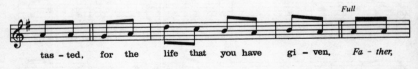

Full

tas - ted, for the life that you have gi - ven, Fa - ther,

Son and Ho - ly Spi - rit, we will praise you.

SECOND TUNE

MAYFIELD

PETER CUTTS (b. 1937)

1. For the bread that we have ea - ten, for the wine that we have

tast - ed, for the life that you have __ giv - en,

REFRAIN

Fa - ther, Son and Ho - ly Spi - rit, we __ will praise you.

After the Lord's Supper

1 For the bread that we have eaten,
  for the wine that we have tasted,
  for the life that you have given,
    Father, Son and Holy Spirit,
    we will praise you.

2 For the life of Christ within us
  turning all our fears to freedom,
  helping us to live for others,
    Father, Son and Holy Spirit,
    we will praise you.

3 For the strength of Christ to lead us
  in our living and our dying,
  in the end, with all your people,
    Father, Son and Holy Spirit,
    we will praise you.

Brian Wren (b. 1936)

25

FORGIVE OUR SINS

American folk-hymn melody from
A Supplement to the Kentucky Harmony (1820)

'For - give our sins as we for - give' you taught us, Lord, to pray,

but you a - lone can grant us grace to live the words we say.

SECOND TUNE

HERMON

Melody, and most of the bass, adapted from
JEREMIAH CLARKE (c. 1673–1707)

'For - give our sins as we ― for - give' you taught us, Lord, to pray,

but you a - lone can grant― us ― grace to live the words we say.

As we forgive. . .

1 'Forgive our sins as we forgive'
    you taught us, Lord, to pray,
  but you alone can grant us grace
    to live the words we say.

2 How can your pardon reach and bless
    the unforgiving heart
  that broods on wrongs and will not let
    old bitterness depart?

3 In blazing light your cross reveals
    the truth we dimly knew,
  how small the debts men owe to us,
    how great our debt to you!

4 Lord, cleanse the depths within our souls
    and bid resentment cease;
  then, reconciled to God and man,
    our lives will spread your peace.

Rosamond E. Herklots (b. 1905)

26
SING HOSANNA

Traditional, arranged by compilers

Refrain (with optional descant)

Sing ho-san - na! Sing ho-san - na! Sing ho-sanna to the king of kings!

Sing ho-san - na! Sing ho-san - na! Sing ho-sanna to the king!

1 Give me joy in my heart, keep me praising,
   give me joy in my heart, I pray;
   give me joy in my heart, keep me praising,
   keep me praising till the break of day.
      Sing hosanna ! Sing hosanna !
      Sing hosanna to the king of kings !
      Sing hosanna ! Sing hosanna !
      Sing hosanna to the king !

2 Give me peace in my heart, keep me loving,
   give me peace in my heart, I pray;
   give me peace in my heart, keep me loving,
   keep me loving till the break of day.

3 Give me love in my heart, keep me serving,
   give me love in my heart, I pray;
   give me love in my heart, keep me serving,
   keep me serving till the break of day.

Traditional

27

GATESCARTH

CARYL MICKLEM (b. 1925)
arranged by compilers

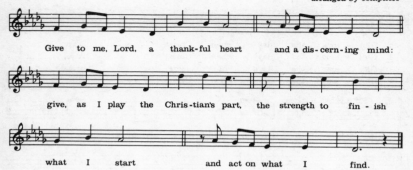

Give to me, Lord, a thank-ful heart and a dis-cern-ing mind:

give, as I play the Chris-tian's part, the strength to fin-ish

what I start and act on what I find.

1 Give to me, Lord, a thankful heart
    and a discerning mind:
  give, as I play the Christian's part,
  the strength to finish what I start
    and act on what I find.

2 When, in the rush of days, my will
    is habit-bound and slow
  help me to keep in vision still
  what love and power and peace can fill
    a life that trusts in you.

3 By your divine and urgent claim
    and by your human face
  kindle our sinking hearts to flame
  and as you teach the world your name
    let it become your place.

4 Jesus, with all your Church I long
    to see your kingdom come:
  show me your way of righting wrong
  and turning sorrow into song
    until you bring me home.

Caryl Micklem (b. 1925)

ILFRACOMBE

JOHN GARDNER (b. 1917)

1. Glor - ious the day when Christ was born _____
2. Glor - ious the day when Christ a - rose, _____
3. Glor - ious the days of gos - pel grace _____
4. Glor - ious the day when Christ ful - fils _____

Al - le - lu - ia, Al - le - lu - ia, Al - le - lu - ia!

to wear the crown that cae - sars scorn, _____
the sur - est Friend of all his foes; _____
when Christ re - stores the fall - en race; _____
what man re - jects yet fee - bly wills; _____

Al - le - lu - ia, Al - le - 'lu - ia, Al - le - lu - ia!

whose life and death that love re - veal _____
who for the sake of those he grieves _____
when doubt - ers kneel and wa - verers stand, _____
when that strong Light puts out the sun _____

Al - le - lu - ia, Al - le - lu - ia, Al - le - lu - ia!

which all men need and need to feel. _____
tran - scends the world he ne - ver leaves. _____
and faith a - chieves what rea - son planned. _____
and all is end - ed, all be - gun _____

Al - le - lu - ia, Al - le - lu - ia, Al - le - lu - ia!

The glorious work of Christ

1 Glorious the day when Christ was born
   Alleluia, Alleluia, Alleluia!
to wear the crown that caesars scorn,
   Alleluia, Alleluia, Alleluia!
whose life and death that love reveal
   Alleluia, Alleluia, Alleluia!
which all men need and need to feel.
   Alleluia, Alleluia, Alleluia!

2 Glorious the day when Christ arose,
the surest Friend of all his foes;
who for the sake of those he grieves
transcends the world he never leaves.

3 Glorious the days of gospel grace
when Christ restores the fallen race;
when doubters kneel and waverers stand,
and faith achieves what reason planned.

4 Glorious the day when Christ fulfils
what man rejects yet feebly wills;
when that strong Light puts out the sun
and all is ended, all begun.

F. Pratt Green (b. 1903)

29

UBI CARITAS

A. GREGORY MURRAY (b. 1905)

REFRAIN

God is love, and where true love ___ is, God him-self is there

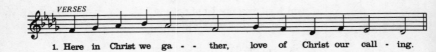

VERSES

1. Here in Christ we ga - - ther, love of Christ our call - ing.

Christ, our love, is with us, glad - ness be his greet - - ing

Let us all re - vere and love him, God e - ter - nal.

Lov - ing him, let each love Christ in all his bro - thers.

Ubi caritas et amor

REFRAIN
   God is love, and where true love is, God himself is there.

1 Here in Christ we gather, love of Christ our calling.
   Christ, our love, is with us, gladness be his greeting.
   Let us all revere and love him, God eternal.
   Loving him, let each love Christ in all his brothers.

   God is love, and where true love is, God himself is there.

2 When we Christians gather, members of one Body,
   let there be in us no discord, but one spirit.
   Banished now be anger, strife and every quarrel.
   Christ, our God, be present always here among us.

   God is love, and where true love is, God himself is there.

3 Grant us love's fulfilment, joy with all the blessed,
   when we see your face, O Saviour, in its glory.
   Shine on us, O purest Light of all creation,
   be our bliss while endless ages sing your praises.

   God is love, and where true love is, God himself is there.

                              James Quinn, S.J. (b. 1919), *altd.*
                              (*from the Liturgy of Maundy Thursday*)

30

THEODORIC

Melody from *Piae Cantiones*, 1582

In moderate time.

Arranged by GUSTAV HOLST (1874–1934)

1. God is love: his the care,

tend-ing each, ev-'ry-where. God is love — all is there!

Je-sus came to show him, that mankind might know him.

Sing a-loud, loud, loud! Sing a-loud, loud, loud!

God is good! God is truth! God is beau-ty! Praise him!

1 God is love: his the care,
   tending each, everywhere.
   God is love—all is there!
      Jesus came to show him,
      that mankind might know him.
         Sing aloud, loud, loud!
         Sing aloud, loud, loud!
         God is good! God is truth!
         God is beauty! Praise him!

2 None can see God above;
   all have here man to love;
   thus may we Godward move,
      finding him in others,
      holding all men brothers.

3 Jesus lived here for men,
   strove and died, rose again,
   rules our hearts, now as then;
      for he came to save us
      by the truth he gave us.

4 To our Lord praise we sing—
   light and life, friend and king,
   coming down love to bring,
      pattern for our duty,
      showing God in beauty.

Percy Dearmer (1867–1936)

31

TURRIFF

ERIC REID (1936–1970)

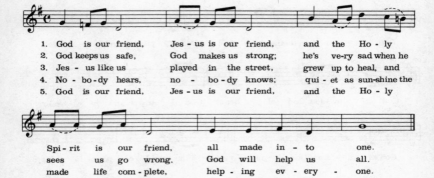

1. God is our friend, Jes - us is our friend, and the Ho - ly
2. God keeps us safe, God makes us strong; he's ve-ry sad when he
3. Jes - us like us played in the street, grew up to heal, and
4. No - bo - dy hears, no - bo - dy knows; qui - et as sun-shine the
5. God is our friend, Jes - us is our friend, and the Ho - ly

Spi - rit is our friend, all made in - to one.
sees us go wrong. God will help us all.
made life com - plete, help - ing ev - ery - one.
Ho - ly Spi - rit goes in - to ev - ery - one.
Spi - rit is our friend, all made in - to one.

1 God is our friend,
   Jesus is our friend,
   and the Holy Spirit is our friend,
   all made into one.

2 God keeps us safe,
   God makes us strong;
   he's very sad when he sees us go wrong.
   God will help us all.

3 Jesus like us
   played in the street,
   grew up to heal, and made life complete,
   helping everyone.

4 Nobody hears,
   nobody knows;
   quiet as sunshine the Holy Spirit goes
   into everyone.

5 God is our friend,
   Jesus is our friend,
   and the Holy Spirit is our friend,
   all made into one.

Eric Reid (1934–70)

CARYL MICKLEM (b. 1925)

God of con - crete, God of steel, God of pis-ton and of wheel,

God of py - lon, God of steam, God of gird-er and of beam,

God of a - tom, God of mine, all the world of power is thine.

'The earth is the Lord's'

1 God of concrete, God of steel,
God of piston and of wheel,
God of pylon, God of steam,
God of girder and of beam,
God of atom, God of mine,
all the world of power is thine.

2 Lord of cable, Lord of rail,
Lord of motorway and mail,
Lord of rocket, Lord of flight,
Lord of soaring satellite,
Lord of lightning's livid line,
all the world of speed is thine.

3 Lord of science, Lord of art,
God of map and graph and chart,
Lord of physics and research,
word of Bible, faith of Church,
Lord of sequence and design,
all the world of truth is thine.

4 God whose glory fills the earth,
gave the universe its birth,
loosed the Christ with Easter's might,
saves the world from evil's blight,
claims mankind by grace divine,
all the world of love is thine.

Richard G. Jones (b. 1926)

CORBRIDGE   ERIK ROUTLEY (b. 1917)

God, who spoke in the be-gin - ning, form-ing rock and shap-ing spar,

set all life & growth in mo - tion, earth-ly world and dis - tant star;

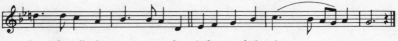

he who calls the earth to or -der is the ground of what ——— we are.

The first and final word

1 God who spoke in the beginning,
    forming rock and shaping spar,
set all life and growth in motion,
    earthly world and distant star;
he who calls the earth to order
    is the ground of what we are.

2 God who spoke through men and nations,
    through events long past and gone,
showing still today his purpose,
    speaks supremely through his Son;
he who calls the earth to order
    gives his word and it is done.

3 God whose speech becomes incarnate
    —Christ is servant, Christ is Lord!—
calls us to a life of service,
    heart and will to action stirred;
he who uses man's obedience
    has the first and final word.

Fred Kaan (b. 1929)

34
SUSSEX

Adapted from an English traditional melody
by R. VAUGHAN WILLIAMS (1872–1958)

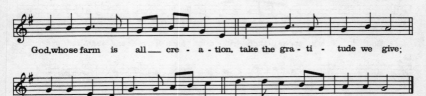

God, whose farm is all — cre - a - tion, take the gra - ti - tude we give;

take the fi - nest of our har - vest, crops we grow that — men may live.

God's farm

1 God, whose farm is all creation,
      take the gratitude we give;
    take the finest of our harvest,
      crops we grow that men may live.

2 Take our ploughing, seeding, reaping,
      hopes and fears of sun and rain,
    all our thinking, planning, waiting,
      ripened in this fruit and grain.

3 All our labour, all our watching,
      all our calendar of care,
    in these crops of your creation,
      take, O God: they are our prayer.

John Arlott (b. 1914)

35

ACH GOTT UND HERR

Melody from *Andachts Zymbeln*, Freiburg, 1655
arranged by JOHANN SEBASTIAN BACH (1685–1750)

Here, Lord, we take the bro-ken bread and drink the wine, be - liev-ing

that by thy life our souls are— fed, thy part-ing gifts— re - ceiv-ing

1 Here, Lord, we take the broken bread
   and drink the wine, believing
   that by thy life our souls are fed,
   thy parting gifts receiving.

2 As thou hast given, so we would give
   ourselves for others' healing;
   as thou hast lived, so we would live,
   the Father's love revealing.

Charles Venn Pilcher (1879–1961)

36

DIEU NOUS AVONS VU

JEAN LANGLAIS (b. 1907)

Organ

Refrain

God, your glo-ry we have seen in your Son, full of truth, full of heav'nly

grace: in Christ make us live, his love shine on our face,

Last time.

and the world will see in us the tri-umph you have won.

Verses

1. In the fields of this world his good news he has sown, and

sends us out to reap till the har-vest is done.

back to Refrain

REFRAIN

God, your glory we have seen in your Son,
full of truth, full of heav'nly grace:
in Christ make us live, his love shine on our face,
and the world will see in us the triumph you have won.

1 In the fields of this world his good news he has sown,
  and sends us out to reap till the harvest is done.
  God, your glory we have seen. . .

2 In his love like a fire that consumes he passed by.
  The flame has touched our lips; let us shout, 'Here am I'.
  God, your glory we have seen. . .

3 He was broken for us, God-forsaken his cry,
  and still the bread he breaks; to ourselves we must die.
  God, your glory we have seen. . .

4 He has trampled the grapes of new life on his cross.
  Now drink the cup and live; he has filled it for us.
  God, your glory we have seen. . .

5 He has founded a kingdom that none shall destroy;
  the corner-stone is laid. Go to work: build with joy!
  God, your glory we have seen. . .

Didier Rimaud
refrain tr. Ronald Johnson (b. 1913)
verses tr. Brian Wren (b. 1936)

37

HAMBLEDEN

WALTER KENDALL STANTON (b. 1891)

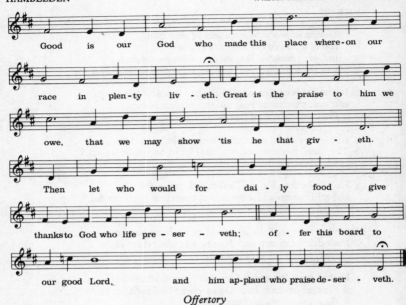

Good is our God who made this place where-on our race in plen-ty liv-eth. Great is the praise to him we owe, that we may show 'tis he that giv - eth. Then let who would for dai - ly food give thanks to God who life pre - ser - veth; of - fer this board to our good Lord, and him ap-plaud who praise de - ser - veth.

Offertory

1 Good is our God who made this place
      whereon our race in plenty liveth.
   Great is the praise to him we owe,
      that we may show 'tis he that giveth.
   Then let who would for daily food
      give thanks to God who life preserveth;
   offer this board to our good Lord,
      and him applaud who praise deserveth.

2 Praise him again whose sovereign will
      grants us the skill of daily labour;
   whose blessed Son to our great good
      fashioned his wood to serve his neighbour.
   Shall we who sing not also bring
      of this world's wages to the Table?—
   giving again of what we gain,
      to make it plain God doth enable.

3 So let us our Creator praise,
      who all our days our life sustaineth;
   offer our work, renew our vow,
      adore him now who rightly reigneth;
   that we who break this bread, and take
      this cup of Christ to our enjoyment,
   may so believe, so well receive,
      never to leave our Lord's employment.

John Gregory (b. 1929)

38

SHEPHERD BOY'S SONG

J. H. ALDEN (b. 1900)

1. He that is down, needs fear no fall,
2. I am con - tent with what I have,
3. Ful - ness to such a bur - den is that

he — that is low, no pride: he that is hum - ble,
lit - tle be — it, or much: and, Lord, con-tent - ment
go — on pil - grim - age: here lit - tle, and here -

e - ver shall have — God to be his guide.
still I crave, be - cause thou sa - vest such.
af - ter bliss, is — best from age to age.

1 He that is down needs fear no fall,
  he that is low, no pride;
  he that is humble ever shall
  have God to be his guide.

2 I am content with what I have,
    little be it, or much:
  and, Lord, contentment still I crave,
    because thou savest such.

3 Fulness to such a burden is
    that go on pilgrimage:
  here little, and hereafter bliss,
    is best from age to age.

John Bunyan (1628–88)

This poem, from Part 2 of *The Pilgrim's Progress*, is the Shepherd-Boy's song in the Valley of Humiliation.

39

WINCHCOMBE   LEONARD BLAKE (b. 1907)

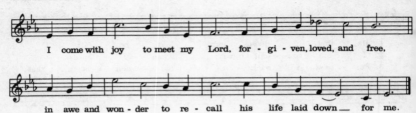

I come with joy to meet my Lord, for - gi - ven, loved, and free,

in awe and won - der to re - call his life laid down __ for me.

Christ making friends

1 I come with joy to meet my Lord,
    forgiven, loved, and free,
  in awe and wonder to recall
    his life laid down for me.

2 I come with Christians far and near,
    to find, as all are fed,
  man's true community of love
    in Christ's communion bread.

3 As Christ breaks bread for men to share
    each proud division ends.
  The love that made us, makes us one,
    and strangers now are friends.

4 And thus with joy we meet our Lord.
    His presence, always near,
  is in such friendship better known:
    we see, and praise him here.

5 Together met, together bound,
    we'll go our different ways,
  and as his people in the world
    we'll live and speak his praise.

Brian Wren (b. 1936)

40

SHRUB END

PETER CUTTS (b. 1937)

Here hangs a man dis-car-ded, a scare-crow hoist-ed high,

a non-sense point-ing no-where to all who hur-ry by.

Last line of V.6

and walk in-to the night.

Hope against hope

I Corinthians 1.18–31

1 Here hangs a man discarded,
   a scarecrow hoisted high,
   a nonsense pointing nowhere
   to all who hurry by.

2 Can such a clown of sorrows
   still bring a useful word
   where faith and love seem phantoms
   and every hope absurd ?

3 Can he give help or comfort
   to lives by comfort bound
   when drums of dazzling progress
   give strangely hollow sound ?

4 Life emptied of all meaning,
   drained out in bleak distress,
   can share in broken silence
   my deepest emptiness ;

5 and love that freely entered
   the pit of life's despair
   can name our hidden darkness
   and suffer with us there.

6 Lord, if you now are risen
   help all who long for light
   to hold the hand of promise
   and walk into the night.

Brian Wren (b. 1936)

41

SHAKER TUNE

Adapted by SYDNEY CARTER (b. 1915)
arranged by JOHN BIRCH (b. 1929)

I danced in the morning when the world was be-gun, and I danced in the moon and the stars and the sun, and I came down from hea-ven and I danced on the earth; at Beth-le-hem I had my birth.

Dance, then, wher-ev-er you may be, I am the Lord of the dance, said he, and I'll lead you all, wher-ev-er you may be, and I'll lead you all in the dance, said he.

Melody of last verse

They cut me down and I leapt up high; I am the life that'll nev-er, ne-ver die; I'll live in you if you'll live in me; I am the Lord of the dance, said he.

Lord of the dance

1 I danced in the morning when the world was begun,
   and I danced in the moon and the stars and the sun,
   and I came down from heaven and I danced on the earth;
   at Bethlehem I had my birth.
   Dance, then, wherever you may be,
   I am the Lord of the dance, said he,
   and I'll lead you all, wherever you may be,
   and I'll lead you all in the dance, said he.

2 I danced for the scribe and the pharisee,
   but they would not dance and they wouldn't follow me.
   I danced for the fishermen, for James and John—
   they came with me and the dance went on.

3 I danced on the Sabbath and I cured the lame;
   the holy people said it was a shame.
   They whipped and they stripped and they hung me on high,
   and they left me there on a cross to die.

4 I danced on a Friday when the sky turned black—
   it's hard to dance with the devil on your back.
   They buried my body and they thought I'd gone,
   but I am the dance, and I still go on.

5 They cut me down and I leapt up high;
   I am the life that'll never, never die;
   I'll live in you if you'll live in me;
   I am the Lord of the dance, said he.

Sydney Carter (b. 1915)

42
WATERLOO

DAVID GOODALL (b. 1922)
arranged by DONALD SWANN, (b. 1923) and compilers

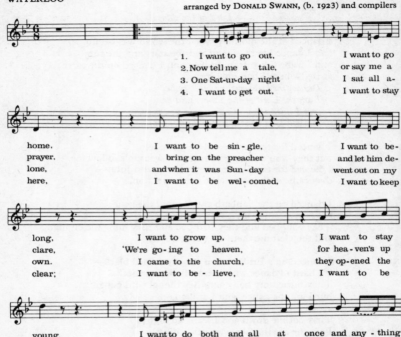

1. I want to go out,   I want to go
2. Now tell me a tale,   or say me a
3. One Sat-ur-day night   I sat all a-
4. I want to get out,   I want to stay

home.   I want to be sin-gle,   I want to be-
prayer.   bring on the preacher   and let him de-
lone,   and when it was Sun-day   went out on my
here,   I want to be wel-comed,   I want to keep

long.   I want to grow up,   I want to stay
clare,   'We're go-ing to heaven,   for hea-ven's up
own.   I came to the church,   they op-ened the
clear;   I want to be-lieve,   I want to be

young,   I want to do both and all at once and any-thing
there.'   But what of the folks who stay be-low and live and
door.   But when I got in the con-gre-ga-tion looked the
sure.   Show me the man who knows the way, the truth, the

else that takes my fan-cy whether it hurts or helps to pass the time of
die and ne-ver re-col-lect the tales they heard in their for-got-ten
same as me and ev-'ry-one as lone-ly as a man with-out a
life and who is yes-ter-day, to-day and ev-er-last-ing-ly the

day: show me the way!
youth?   Tell them the truth!
wife,   look-ing for life.
same;   tell me his name!

Song for a not-quite-converted Christian

1 I want to go out,
   I want to go home,
   I want to be single,
   I want to belong,
   I want to grow up,
   I want to stay young,
   I want to do both and all at once and anything else that
       takes my fancy whether it hurts or helps to pass the
       time of day:
   show me the way!

2 Now tell me a tale,
   or say me a prayer,
   bring on the preacher
   and let him declare,
   'We're going to heaven,
   for heaven's up there'.
   But what of the folks who stay below and live and die and
       never recollect the tales they heard in their
       forgotten youth?
   Tell them the truth!

3 One Saturday night
   I sat all alone,
   and when it was Sunday
   went out on my own.
   I came to the church,
   they opened the door.
   But when I got in the congregation looked the same as me
       and everyone as lonely as a man without a wife,
   looking for life.

4 I want to get out,
   I want to stay here,
   I want to be welcomed,
   I want to keep clear;
   I want to believe,
   I want to be sure.
   Show me the man who knows the way, the truth, the life
       and who is yesterday, today and everlastingly the same;
   tell me his name!

                                    David Goodall (b. 1922)

43

ACKERGILL   LEONARD BLAKE (b. 1907)

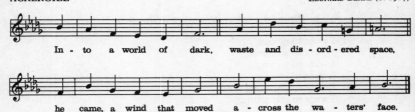

In - to a world of dark, waste and dis - ord - ered space,

he came, a wind that moved a - cross the wa - ters' face.

1 Into a world of dark,
    waste and disordered space,
  he came, a wind that moved
    across the waters' face.

2 The Spirit in the wild
    breathed, and a world began.
  From shapelessness came form,
    from nothingness, a plan.

3 Light in the darkness grew;
    land in the water stood;
  and space and time became
    a beauty that was good.

4 Into a world of doubt,
    through doors we closed, he came,
  the breath of God in power
    like wind and roaring flame.

5 From empty wastes of death
    on love's disordered grief
  light in the darkness blazed
    and kindled new belief.

6 Still, with creative power,
    God's Spirit gives to men
  a pattern of new life—
    and worlds begin again.

Ann Phillips (b. 1930)
and compilers

44

CHEREPONI

Melody from N. Ghana, harmonised by compilers

Refrain

Je - su, _____ Je - su, _____ fill us with your love, show us how to serve the neighbours we have from you. _____ *Fine*

Verses

Kneels at the feet of his friends, si - lent - ly wash - es their feet,

Mas - ter who acts as a slave _____ to them. _____

REFRAIN

Jesu, Jesu,
fill us with your love,
show us how to serve
the neighbours we have from you.

1 Kneels at the feet of his friends,
silently washes their feet,
Master who acts as a slave to them.
Jesu, Jesu...

2 Neighbours are rich men and poor,
neighbours are black men and white,
neighbours are nearby and far away.
Jesu, Jesu...

3 These are the ones we should serve,
these are the ones we should love.
All men are neighbours to us and you.
Jesu, Jesu...

4 Kneel at the feet of our friends,
silently washing their feet,
this is the way we should live with you.
Jesu, Jesu...

from N. Ghana

It is suggested that in singing this hymn 'Jesu' should be pronounced 'Yay-soo', as in Greek, Latin, French, German, etc.

45

AU CLAIR DE LA LUNE

Old French melody

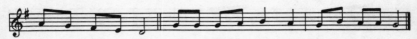

1 Jesus' hands were kind hands, doing good to all,
   healing pain and sickness, blessing children small,
   washing tired feet and saving those who fall.
   Jesus' hands were kind hands, doing good to all.

2 Take my hands, Lord Jesus, let them work for you.
   Make them strong and gentle, kind in all I do.
   Let me watch you, Jesus, till I'm gentle too;
   till my hands are kind hands, quick to work for you.

Margaret Cropper (b. 1886)

46

PETERSFIELD

WILLIAM H. HARRIS (1883–1973)

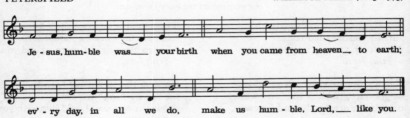

Christ in us

1 Jesus, humble was your birth
   when you came from heaven to earth;
   every day, in all we do,
   make us humble, Lord, like you.

2 Jesus, strong to help and heal,
   showing that your love is real;
   every day, in all we do,
   make us strong and kind like you.

3 Jesus, when you were betrayed
   still you trusted God and prayed;
   every day, in all we do,
   help us trust and pray like you.

4 Jesus, risen from the dead,
   with us always, as you said;
   every day, in all we do,
   help us live and love like you.

Patrick Appleford (b. 1924), *altd.*

The original tune to these words—'Catherine' by Gerard Beaumont C.R.—is to be found in *Twenty-Seven 20th Century Hymns*, published by Josef Weinberger Ltd.

47

YISU NE KAHA

Urdu melody
harmonised by FRANCIS WESTBROOK (b. 1903)

The voice of Jesus

1 Jesus the Lord says, I am the bread,
the bread of life for mankind am I.
    The bread of life for mankind am I,
    the bread of life for mankind am I.
Jesus the Lord says, I am the bread,
the bread of life for mankind am I.

2 Jesus the Lord says, I am the way,
the true and living way am I.

3 Jesus the Lord says, I am the light,
the one true light of the world am I.

4 Jesus the Lord says, I am the shepherd,
the one good shepherd of the sheep am I.

5 Jesus the Lord says, I am the life,
the resurrection and the life am I.

Anonymous,
tr. from the Urdu by Dermott Monahan (1906–57), altd.

48

EMLEY MOOR

PETER CUTTS (b. 1937)

Joy wings to God our song, _____ for all life holds _____ to stir the heart, _____ to light the mind and make_____ our spi – rit strong.

CAERLAVEROCK

CARYL MICKLEM (b. 1925)

Joy wings to God our song, for all _____ life holds to stir the heart, to light the mind and make_____ our spi – rit strong.

1 Joy wings to God our song,
    for all life holds
    to stir the heart,
    to light the mind
    and make our spirit strong.

2 Joy wings our grateful hymn,
    for home and friends
    and all the love
    that fills our cup
    of gladness to the brim.

3 Joy wings to God our praise,
    for wisdom's wealth,
    our heritage
    from every age,
    to guide us in his ways.

4 Joy wings to God our prayer.
    All gifts we need
    of courage, faith,
    forgiveness, peace,
    are offered by his care.

5 Joy wings our heart and voice
    to give ourselves
    to Christ who died
    and, risen, lives
    that we may all rejoice.

Albert Frederick Bayly (b. 1901)

49

KUM BA YAH

Traditional tune
harmonised by compilers

1 Kum ba yah, my Lord,
2 Some-one's cry - ing, Lord,
3 Some-one's sing - ing, Lord,
4 Some-one's pray - ing, Lord,
kum ba yah!

Kum ba
Some-one's
Some-one's
Some-one's

yah, my Lord,
cry - ing, Lord,
sing - ing, Lord,
pray - ing, Lord,
kum ba yah!

Kum ba yah, my Lord,
Some-one's cry - ing Lord,
Some-one's sing - ing Lord,
Some-one's pray - ing Lord,
kum ba

yah. _____ O Lord, _____ kum ba yah.

1 Kum ba yah, my Lord, kum ba yah!
Kum ba yah, my Lord, kum ba yah!
Kum ba yah, my Lord, kum ba yah!
    O Lord, kum ba yah!

2 Someone's crying, Lord, kum ba yah!. . .

3 Someone's singing, Lord, kum ba yah!. . .

4 Someone's praying, Lord, kum ba yah!. . .   *Traditional*

'Kum ba yah' may be a 'pidgin-English' corruption of 'Come by here'

50

LET THE COSMOS RING

JACK GREEN

REFRAIN

Let the cos - mos ring, _____ as we clap and
sing for Je - sus Christ our King. Let the cosmos ring, _____
_____ as we clap and sing for Je - sus Christ our ___ King.

Full

Praise him! _____ Praise him! _____

Solo

1. With the tap of the type - wri - ter, with the
2. With the shout of a news - boy. with the
3. With the laugh of a show - girl, with a

Praise him! _____

honk of a horn, _____ in the wet win-dy wea - ther,
rumble of trains, in the tow-er-ing build - ings,
folk artist's song, in a tum-bledown shan - ty,

Praise him! _____ REFRAIN

in the dawn new-ly born.)
in the dark al - ley-ways. }   Let the cos - mos ring,
on the fresh-ly mown lawn.)

The verses are best taken antiphonally, the main company singing 'Praise him' (and
holding the last note each time), and a leader or group singing 'with the tap of the
typewriter' etc. Further verses can be added.

REFRAIN

Let the cosmos ring,
as we clap and sing for Jesus Christ our King.
Let the cosmos ring,
as we clap and sing for Jesus Christ our King.

1 Praise him!
   with the tap of the typewriter.
Praise him!
   with the honk of a horn.
Praise him!
   in the wet windy weather.
Praise him!
   in the dawn newly born.
     Let the cosmos ring. . .

2 Praise him!
   with the shout of a newsboy.
Praise him!
   with the rumble of trains.
Praise him!
   in the towering buildings.
Praise him!
   in the dark alleyways.
     Let the cosmos ring. . .

3 Praise him!
   with the laugh of a showgirl.
Praise him!
   with a folk artist's song.
Praise him!
   in a tumbledown shanty.
Praise him!
   on the freshly mown lawn.
              Valerie Dunn

51

JONATHAN

ROBIN SHELDON (b. 1932)

Life has ma-ny rhy-thms, ev-ery heart its beat;

ev-ery-where we hear the sound of danc-ing feet.

Life is this world's sec-ret; Lord of life, for-give,

if we ne-ver asked you what it means to live.

OPTIONAL DESCANT FOR VERSE 4

Life is meant for lo-ving. Lord, if this is true, love of life and

neighbour spring from love of you. Give us your com-pas-sion: yours

the name we bear; yours the on-ly vic'try we would serve and share.

Dialogue

1 Life has many rhythms, every heart its beat;
everywhere we hear the sound of dancing feet.
Life is this world's secret: Lord of life, forgive,
if we never asked you what it means to live.

2 *Life is meant for loving.* Lord, if this is true,
why do millions suffer without help from you?
Some who fought injustice added wrong to wrong:
can it be that love is stronger than the strong?

3 It was you who promised: *All who seek shall find.*
What we find lies deeper than our reach of mind;
what we found was you, Lord, you the God above,
you had come, as Victim, to the world you love!

4 *Life is meant for loving.* Lord, if this is true,
love of life and neighbour spring from love of you.
Give us your compassion: yours the name we bear;
yours the only victory we would serve and share.

F. Pratt Green (b. 1903)

52
LITHEROP

PETER CUTTS (b. 1937)

Life is great! So sing a-bout it, as we can and as we should —

shops and bus - es, towns and peo - ple, vil-lage, farm-land, field and wood.

V.5

Life is great and life is gi - ven. Life is love - ly, free and good.

A song of love and living

1 Life is great! So sing about it,
 as we can and as we should—
 shops and buses, towns and people,
 village, farmland, field and wood.
 Life is great and life is given.
 Life is lovely, free and good.

2 Life is great!—whatever happens,
 snow or sunshine, joy or pain,
 hardship, grief or disillusion,
 suffering that I can't explain—
 life is great if someone loves me,
 holds my hand and calls my name.

3 Love is great!—the love of lovers,
 whispered words and longing eyes;
 love that gazes at the cradle
 where a child of loving lies;
 love that lasts when youth has faded,
 bends with age, but never dies.

4 Love is giving and receiving—
 boy and girl, or friend with friend.
 Love is bearing and forgiving
 all the hurts that hate can send.
 Love's the greatest way of living,
 hoping, trusting to the end.

5 God is great! In Christ he loved us,
 as we should, but never can—
 love that suffered, hoped and trusted
 when disciples turned and ran,
 love that broke through death for ever.
 Praise that loving, living Man!

Brian Wren (b. 1936)

53

WANSBECK

ERIK ROUTLEY (b. 1917)

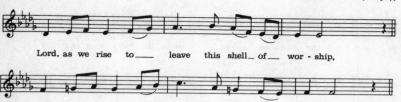

Lord, as we rise to___ leave this shell___ of___ wor-ship,

called to the risk of___ un - pro - tec - ted___ liv - ing,

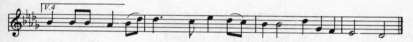

Vv 1-3

will-ing to be at___ one with all your___ peo-ple, we ask for cour-age.

V.4

be with your church in death and re - sur - rec-tion, Lord of all a - ges.

Into the world

1 Lord, as we rise to leave this shell of worship,
  called to the risk of unprotected living,
  willing to be at one with all your people,
      we ask for courage.

2 For all the strain with living interwoven,
  for the demands each day will make upon us,
  and for the love we owe the modern city,
      Lord, make us cheerful.

3 Give us an eye for openings to serve you;
  make us alert when calm is interrupted,
  ready and wise to use the unexpected:
      sharpen our insight.

4 Lift from our life the blanket of convention;
  give us the nerve to lose our life to others;
  be with your church in death and resurrection,
      Lord of all ages.

Fred Kaan (b. 1929)

54

RAWTHORPE

PETER CUTTS (b. 1937)

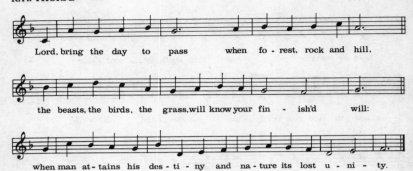

Lord, bring the day to pass when fo - rest, rock and hill,

the beasts, the birds, the grass, will know your fin - ish'd will:

when man at - tains his des - ti - ny and na - ture its lost u - ni - ty.

1 Lord, bring the day to pass
   when forest, rock and hill,
the beasts, the birds, the grass,
   will know your finished will:
when man attains his destiny
and nature its lost unity.

2 Forgive our careless use
   of water, ore and soil—
the plenty we abuse
   supplied by others' toil:
save us from making self our creed,
turn us towards our brother's need.

3 Give us, when we release
   creation's secret powers,
to harness them for peace—
   our children's peace and ours:
teach us the art of mastering
which makes life rich and draws death's sting.

4 Creation groans, travails,
   futile its present plight,
bound—till the hour it hails
   the newfound sons of light
who enter on their true estate.
Come, Lord: new heavens and earth create.

Ian Fraser (b. 1917)

55

HAMPTON POYLE

PETER CUTTS (b. 1937)

Lord Christ, the Fa-ther's might-y Son, _____ whose work up-on the cross was done all men to re-ceive, make all our scat-tered chur-ches one that the world may be-lieve.

Christian unity

1 Lord Christ, the Father's mighty Son,
  whose work upon the cross was done
    all men to receive,
  make all our scattered churches one
    that the world may believe.

2 To make us one your prayers were said.
  To make us one you broke the bread
    for all to receive.
  Its pieces scatter us instead:
    how can others believe?

3 Lord Christ, forgive us, make us new!
  What our designs could never do
    your love can achieve.
  Our prayers, our work, we bring to you
    that the world may believe.

4 We will not question or refuse
  the way you work, the means you choose,
    the pattern you weave,
  but reconcile our warring views
    that the world may believe.

Brian Wren (b. 1936)

ABINGDON

ERIK ROUTLEY (b. 1917)

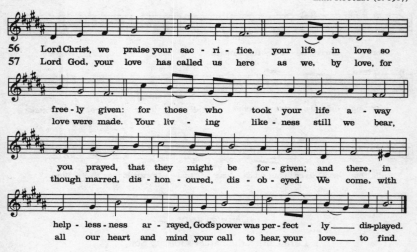

56 Lord Christ, we praise your sac - ri - fice, your life in love so
57 Lord God, your love has called us here as we, by love, for

free - ly given: for those who took your life a - way
love were made. Your liv - ing like - ness still we bear,

you prayed, that they might be for - given; and there, in
though marred, dis - hon - oured, dis - ob - eyed. We come, with

help - less - ness ar - rayed, God's power was per - fect - ly ___ dis - played.
all our heart and mind your call to hear, your love ___ to find.

56

1 Lord Christ, we praise your sacrifice,
    your life in love so freely given:
for those who took your life away
    you prayed, that they might be
                        [forgiven;
and there, in helplessness arrayed,
God's power was perfectly displayed.

2 Once helpless in your mother's arms,
    dependent on her mercy then,
you made yourself again, by choice,
    as helpless in the hands of men;
and, at their mercy crucified,
you claimed your victory and died.

3 Though helpless and rejected then,
    you're now as reigning Lord acclaimed;
for ever by your victory
    is God's eternal love proclaimed—
the love which goes through death to find
new life and hope for all mankind.

4 So, living Lord, prepare us now
    your willing helplessness to share;
to give ourselves in sacrifice
    to overcome the world's despair;
in love to give our lives away
and claim your victory today.

Alan Gaunt (b. 1935)

57

'And can it be. . .

1 Lord God, your love has called us here
    as we, by love, for love were made.
Your living likeness still we bear,
    though marred, dishonoured, disobeyed.
We come, with all our heart and mind
your call to hear, your love to find.

2 We come with self-inflicted pains
    of broken trust and chosen wrong,
half-free, half-bound by inner chains,
    by social forces swept along,
by powers and systems close confined
yet seeking hope for all mankind.

3 Lord God, in Christ you call our name
    and then receive us as your own
not through some merit, right or claim
    but by your gracious love alone.
We strain to glimpse your mercy-seat
and find you kneeling at our feet.

4 Then take the towel, and break the bread,
    and humble us, and call us friends.
Suffer and serve till all are fed,
    and show how grandly love intends
to work till all creation sings,
to fill all worlds, to crown all things.

5 Lord God, in Christ you set us free
    your life to live, your joy to share.
Give us your Spirit's liberty
    to turn from guilt and dull despair
and offer all that faith can do
while love is making all things new.

Brian Wren (b. 1936)

58

CITY OF GOD

DANIEL MOE (b. 1924)

1. Lord Je-sus, if I love and serve my neigh-bour out of my
2. When I have met my bro-ther's need with kind - ness and prayed that
3. Lord, though I cling to safe - ty or pos - sess - ions, yet from the

knowledge, lei - sure, power or wealth, o - pen my eyes to understand his
he could wa - ken from des - pair, o - pen my ears if, crying now for
cross love's pov - er - ty pre - vails: o - pen my heart to life and lib - er-

an - ger if from his help - less - ness he hates my help.
jus - tice, he strug - gles for the chan - ges that I fear.
- a - tion, o - pen my hands to bear the mark of nails.

Pilgrimage of confession

1 Lord Jesus, if I love and serve my neighbour
   out of my knowledge, leisure, power or wealth,
   open my eyes to understand his anger
      if from his helplessness he hates my help.

2 When I have met my brother's need with kindness
   and prayed that he could waken from despair,
   open my ears if, crying now for justice,
      he struggles for the changes that I fear.

3 Lord, though I cling to safety or possessions,
   yet from the cross love's poverty prevails:
   open my heart to life and liberation,
      open my hands to bear the mark of nails.

Brian Wren (b. 1936)

59

FRANCONIA

W. H. HAVERGAL (1793–1870), adapted from a tune in KONIG'S *Harmonischer Liederschatz* (1738) (harmony slightly altered)

Lord Je-sus, once a child, Sav-iour of young and old, re-ceive this lit-tle child of ours in-to your flock and fold.

Christian baptism

1 Lord Jesus, once a child,
   Saviour of young and old,
   receive this little child of ours
   into your flock and fold.

2 You drank the cup of life,
   its bitterness and bliss,
   and loved us to the uttermost
   for such a child as this.

3 So help us, Lord, to trust,
   through this baptismal rite,
   not in our own imperfect love,
   but in your saving might.

F. Pratt Green (b. 1903), *altd.*

60

SAN ROCCO

Derek Williams (b. 1945)

Lord of the bound-less curves of space and time's deep mys-te-ry,

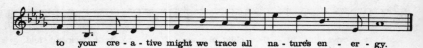

to your cre-a-tive might we trace all na-ture's en-er-gy.

A hymn of the universe

1 Lord of the boundless curves of space
   and time's deep mystery,
   to your creative might we trace
   all nature's energy.

2 Your mind conceived the galaxy,
   each atom's secret planned,
   and every age of history
   your purpose, Lord, has spanned.

3 Your Spirit gave the living cell
   its hidden, vital force:
   the instincts which all life impel
   derive from you, their source.

4 You gave the growing consciousness
   that flowered at last in man,
   with all his longing to progress,
   discover, shape and plan.

5 In Christ the living power of grace
   to liberate and lead
   lights up the future of our race
   with mercy's crowning deed.

6 Lead us, whom love has made and sought,
   to find, when planets fall,
   that Omega of life and thought
   where Christ is all in all.

Albert Frederick Bayly (b. 1901)
and Brian Wren (b. 1936)

61

GLENCAPLE

CARYL MICKLEM (b. 1925)

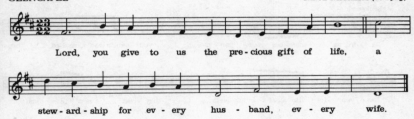

Lord, you give to us the pre-cious gift of life, a
stew-ard-ship for ev-ery hus-band, ev-ery wife.

1 Lord, you give to us
   the precious gift of life,
   a stewardship for every husband, every wife.

2 Lord, you give to us
   not only flesh and blood,
   but mind and heart and soul to know that they are good.

3 Lord, you offer us
   the water, bread and wine.
   By faith we reach out for your love within the sign.

4 Lord, you offer us
   new life that never ends—
   you suffer, serve, and die, and live to call us friends.

5 Lord, you ask of us
   a death to what we knew.
   Then, rising in your name, we'll put our trust in you.

6 Lord, you share with us
   our hope for what will be.
   With us prepare each child by love, your love to see.

Stephen Orchard (b. 1942)
and compilers

A SONG OF PRAISE FOR ALL THE SAINTS

DOREEN NEWPORT (b. 1927)

Semichorus

1. Lord, we re-mem-ber your peo-ple, ____ your saints who have died; ____ they loved you in life and in death, ____ they rest ____ now in you.

ALL *(Refrain follows each verse)*

Thanks be to God for his saints: they call ____ us to fol – low Christ our Lord.

2. Through a - ges of dark - ness and sor - row ____ they clung ____ to you, Lord; in pri - son and dan - ger they found you, ____ your will was their ____ peace.

3 Re - joic - ing in you, Lord, they flourished, ____ their lives sang your praise; ____ you gave them your bread and your bless - ing, ____ you held ____ them in love.

4 Lord, we re - mem - ber your peo - ple, ____ we fol - low their way; ____ our prais - es are joined with their prais - es, ____ keep us ____ faith - ful to you.

Judith O'Neill

63
STONER HILL

WILLIAM H. HARRIS (1883–1973)

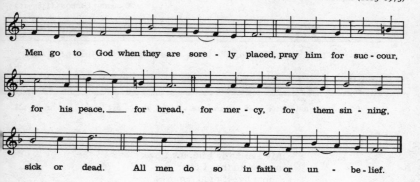

Men go to God when they are sore - ly placed, pray him for suc - cour,

for his peace,___ for bread, for mer - cy, for them sin - ning,

sick or dead. All men do so in faith or un - be - lief.

1 Men go to God when they are sorely placed,
  pray him for succour, for his peace, for bread,
  for mercy for them sinning, sick or dead.
  All men do so in faith or unbelief.

2 Men go to God when he is sorely placed,
  find him poor, scorned, unsheltered, without bread,
  whelmed under weight of evil, weak or dead.
  Christians stand by God in his hour of grief.

3 God goes to man when he is sorely placed,
  body and spirit feeds he with his bread.
  For every man, he as a man hangs dead:
  forgiven life he gives men through his death.

Dietrich Bonhoeffer (1906–45),
versified by W. H. Farquharson

64

SONG 20

Melody and most of the bass by
ORLANDO GIBBONS (1583–1625)

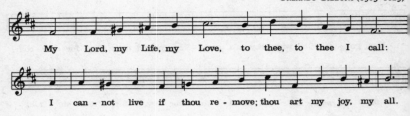

My Lord, my Life, my Love, to thee, to thee I call:

I can-not live if thou re-move; thou art my joy, my all.

1 My Lord, my Life, my Love,
   to thee, to thee I call:
   I cannot live if thou remove;
   thou art my joy, my all.

2 My only sun to cheer
   the darkness where I dwell;
   the best and only true delight
   my song hath found to tell.

3 To thee in very heaven
   the angels owe their bliss,
   to thee the saints, whom thou hast called
   where perfect pleasure is.

4 And how shall man, thy child,
   without thee happy be,
   who hath no comfort nor desire
   in all the world but thee?

5 Return, my Love, my Life,
   thy grace hath won my heart;
   if thou forgive, if thou return,
   I will no more depart.

Robert Bridges (1844–1930)
based on a hymn by Isaac Watts (1674–1748)

65

ST BARTHOLOMEW

HENRY DUNCALF (d. 1762)
(from W. RILEY'S *Parochial Harmony*, 1762)

My God, my king, thy va - rious praise shall fill the rem-nant of __ my days

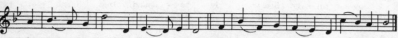

thy grace __ em-ploy my hum - ble tongue till death __ and glo - ry raise the song.

OPTIONAL DESCANT FOR V.5

arranged by JOHN WILSON

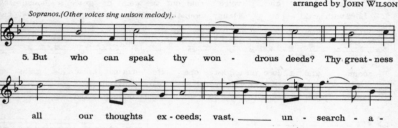

Sopranos.(Other voices sing unison melody)..

5. But who can speak thy won - drous deeds? Thy great - ness

all our thoughts ex - ceeds; vast, _____ un - search - a -

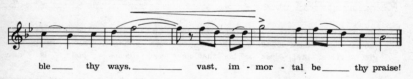

ble __ thy ways, _____ vast, im - mor - tal be ____ thy praise!

The greatness of God

1 My God, my king, thy various praise
   shall fill the remnant of my days;
   thy grace employ my humble tongue,
   till death and glory raise the song.

2 The wings of every hour shall bear
   some thankful tribute to thine ear,
   and every setting sun shall see
   new works of duty done for thee.

3 Thy truth and justice I'll proclaim;
   thy bounty flows, an endless stream;
   thy mercy swift; thine anger slow,
   but dreadful to the stubborn foe.

4 Let distant times and nations raise
   the long succession of thy praise;
   and unborn ages make my song
   the joy and labour of their tongue.

5 But who can speak thy wondrous deeds?
   Thy greatness all our thoughts exceeds;
   vast and unsearchable thy ways,
   vast and immortal be thy praise.

Isaac Watts (1674–1748),
based on Psalm 145

66

GENEVAN PSALM 98
(RENDEZ A DIEU)

Melody from *La Forme des Prieres et*
Chants Ecclesiastiques (Strasbourg, 1545)
(2nd line as in *Genevan Psalter* of 1551)

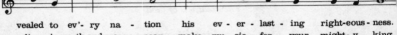

1 New songs of ce - le - bra - tion ren - der to him who
2 Joy - ful - ly, heart - i - ly re - sound - ing, let ev' - ry
3 Ri - vers and seas and tor - rents roar - ing, hon - our the

has great won - ders done. Love sits en-throned in age - less splend - our:
in - stru - ment and voice peal out the praise of grace a - bound - ing,
Lord with wild ac - claim; moun-tains and stones look up a - dor - ing

come and a - dore the might-y one. He has made known his great sal-
call - ing the whole world to re - joice. Trum-pets and or - gans, set in
and find a voice to praise his name. Right-eous, com-mand - ing, ev - er

va - tion which all his friends with joy con - fess: he has re -
mo - tion such sounds as make the hea - vens ring; all things that
glo - rious, prai - ses be his that ne - ver cease: just is our

vealed to ev' - ry na - tion his ev - er - last - ing right-eous - ness.
live in earth and o - cean, make mu - sic for your might - y king.
God, whose truth vic - tor - ious es - tab - lish - es the world in peace.

1 New songs of celebration render
   to him who has great wonders done.
Love sits enthroned in ageless splendour:
   come and adore the mighty one.
He has made known his great salvation
   which all his friends with joy confess:
he has revealed to every nation
   his everlasting righteousness.

2 Joyfully, heartily resounding,
   let every instrument and voice
peal out the praise of grace abounding,
   calling the whole world to rejoice.
Trumpets and organs, set in motion
   such sounds as make the heavens ring;
all things that live in earth and ocean,
   make music for your mighty king.

3 Rivers and seas and torrents roaring,
   honour the Lord with wild acclaim;
mountains and stones look up adoring
   and find a voice to praise his name.
Righteous, commanding, ever glorious,
   praises be his that never cease:
just is our God, whose truth victorious
   establishes the world in peace.

Erik Routley (b. 1917)
tr. from 1970 revision of the French Psalter

67

S. S. Wesley (1810–76)

Not far be - yond the sea, nor high a - bove the heavens, but ve - ry nigh

thy voice, O God, is heard. For each new step of faith we take

thou hast more truth and light to— break forth from thy ho - ly word.

Truth and light

1 Not far beyond the sea, nor high
   above the heavens, but very nigh
     thy voice, O God, is heard.
   For each new step of faith we take
   thou hast more truth and light to break
     forth from thy holy word.

2 Rooted and grounded in thy love,
   with saints on earth and saints above
     we join in full accord
   to grasp the breadth, length, depth and height,
   the crucified and risen might
     of Christ, the incarnate Word.

3 Help us to press toward that mark,
   and, though our vision now is dark,
     to live by what we see.
   So, when we see thee face to face,
   thy truth and light our dwelling-place
     for evermore shall be.

George Bradford Caird (b. 1917)

68

JOHN ONE

CARYL MICKLEM (b. 1925)

No one has ev - er seen God; but God's on - ly Son,

he who is near-est to the Fath - er's heart, he has made him — known.

John 1 . 18, New English Bible

Each of these single-verse hymns is meant to be sung (by choir or congregation) as a response to spoken prayer or reading, perhaps repeated several times in the course of a service or of one act of prayer within it. See also 3.

69

EDMONDSHAM

JOHN H. LORING (b. 1906)

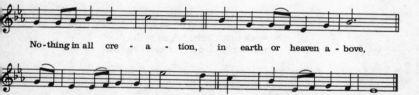

No - thing in all cre - a - tion, in earth or heaven a - bove,

can come be - tween God's peo - ple and God's e - ter - nal love.

Par. by CARYL MICKLEM (b. 1925) from *Romans* 8 . 38-9

70

SOLOTHURN

Swiss traditional melody

Now let us from this tab - le rise re-newed in bo - dy, mind and soul;

with Christ we die and live a - gain, his self - less love has made us whole.

After the Lord's Supper

1 Now let us from this table rise
   renewed in body, mind and soul;
   with Christ we die and live again,
   his selfless love has made us whole.

2 With minds alert, upheld by grace,
   to spread the Word in speech and deed,
   we follow in the steps of Christ,
   at one with man in hope and need.

3 To fill each human house with love,
   it is the sacrament of care;
   the work that Christ began to do
   we humbly pledge ourselves to share.

4 Then grant us courage, father God,
   to choose again the pilgrim way,
   and help us to accept with joy
   the challenge of tomorrow's day.

Fred Kaan (b. 1929)

71

GEOFFREY LAYCOCK

Now join we, to praise the cre - a - tor, our voi - ces in
wor - ship and song; we stand to re - call with thanks-
giv - ing that to him all sea - sons be - long.

Harvest

1 Now join we, to praise the creator,
   our voices in worship and song;
   we stand to recall with thanksgiving
   that to him all seasons belong.

2 We thank you, O God, for your goodness,
   for the joy and abundance of crops,
   for food that is stored in our larders,
   for all we can buy in the shops.

3 But also of need and starvation
   we sing with concern and despair—
   of skills that are used for destruction,
   of land that is burnt and laid bare.

4 We cry for the plight of the hungry
   while harvests are left on the field,
   for orchards neglected and wasting,
   for produce from markets withheld.

5 The song grows in depth and in wideness:
   the earth and its people are one.
   There can be no thanks without giving,
   no words without deeds that are done.

6 Then teach us, O Lord of the harvest,
   to be humble in all that we claim;
   to share what we have with the nations,
   to care for the world in your name.

Fred Kaan (b. 1929)

72

QUITTEZ, PASTEURS

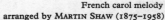
French carol melody
arranged by MARTIN SHAW (1875–1958)

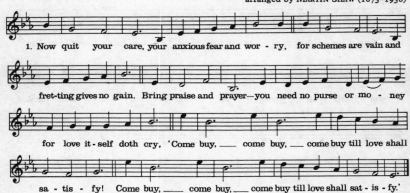

1. Now quit your care, your anxious fear and wor - ry, for schemes are vain and fret-ting gives no gain. Bring praise and prayer—you need no purse or mo - ney for love it - self doth cry, 'Come buy, ___ come buy, ___ come buy till love shall sa - tis - fy! Come buy, ___ come buy, ___ come buy till love shall sat - is - fy.'

1 Now quit your care,
    for anxious fear and worry,
      your schemes are vain
      and fretting gives no gain.
    Bring praise and prayer—
      you need no purse or money
      for love itself doth cry,
        'Come buy, come buy,
        come buy, till love shall satisfy'.

2 To bow the head
    in sackcloth and in ashes,
      or rend the soul,
      such grief is not our goal;
    but to be led
      to where God's glory flashes,
      his beauty to come nigh,
        to fly, to fly,
        to fly where truth and light do lie.

3 For is not this
    the fast that I have chosen
      (the prophet spoke)
      to shatter every yoke,
    of wickedness
      the grievous bands to loosen,
      oppression put to flight,
        to fight, to fight,
        to fight till every wrong's set right?

4 For righteousness
    and peace will show their faces
      to those who feed
      the hungry in their need,
    and wrongs redress,
      who build the old waste places,
      and in the darkness shine.
        Divine, divine,
        divine it is when all combine!

5 Then shall your light
    break forth as doth the morning;
      your health shall spring,
      the friends you make shall bring
    God's glory bright,
      your way through life adorning;
      and love shall be the prize.
        Arise, arise,
        arise! and make a paradise!

Percy Dearmer (1867–1936), altd.

The words, written for the carol 'Quittez, Pasteurs', are in part a paraphrase of the Lent lesson, Isaiah lviii. Verses 1 and 2 have been altered by Brian Wren to make it a hymn for all seasons.

73

WOODMANSTERNE

CARYL MICKLEM (b. 1925)

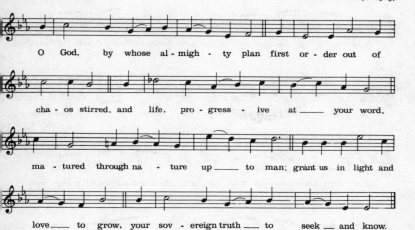

O God, by whose al-migh-ty plan first or-der out of cha-os stirred, and life, pro-gress-ive at ___ your word, ma-tured through na-ture up ___ to man; grant us in light and love ___ to grow, your sov-ereign truth ___ to seek ___ and know.

The healing God

1 O God, by whose almighty plan
first order out of chaos stirred,
and life, progressive at your word,
matured through nature up to man;
   grant us in light and love to grow,
   your sovereign truth to seek and know.

2 O Christ, whose touch unveiled the blind,
whose presence warmed the lonely soul;
your love made broken sinners whole,
your faith cast devils from the mind.
   Grant us your faith, your love, your care
   to bring to sufferers everywhere.

3 O Holy Spirit, by whose grace
our skills abide, our wisdom grows,
in every healing work disclose
new paths to probe, new thoughts to trace.
   Grant us your wisest way to go
   in all we think, or speak, or do.

H. C. A. Gaunt (b. 1902)

74

ASKERSWELL

PETER CUTTS (b. 1937)

Once from a Eu-ro-pe-an shore men sailed to find and rule the earth,

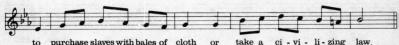

to purchase slaves with bales of cloth or take a ci-vi-li-zing law.

Give thanks that some up-on that tide, with faith and fail-ings like our own,

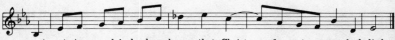

went out to preach in lands un-known that Christ___ for ev'-ry man had died.

World Church, World Mission

1 Once from a European shore
    men sailed to find and rule the earth,
    to purchase slaves with bales of cloth
or take a civilizing law.
Give thanks that some upon that tide,
    with faith and failings like our own,
    went out to preach in lands unknown
that Christ for every man had died.

2 Give thanks that with the tangled strands
    of empire, honour, greed and love
    a single world God's Spirit wove
from earth's long-separated lands.
And now that all mankind must face
    the dread and hope of being one
    give thanks again that Christ is known
in every continent and race.

3 Still in this shrinking world men crave
    a nation's glory, might or gain,
    and unshared wealth, unheeded pain
divide the master from the slave.
Give thanks that some yet hear the call
    and find in Christ a love to span
    the bitter chasms made by man
and break each new dividing wall.

4 A great community of hope
    by reconciling love reborn
    today from all the earth is drawn—
God's pageant and kaleidoscope.
Give thanks that treasures long prepared
    —the wisdom, insight, gifts and grace
    of every culture, age and place—
in Christ can now be seen and shared.

5 Lord, open out our heart and mind
    to glimpse what still the Church could be—
    a source of hope and unity,
a prototype for all mankind.
Help us to honour, trust and serve
    each unknown friend that Christ has made.
    Give us a hope that does not fade,
to build a world of peace and love.

Brian Wren (b. 1936)

75

TRANSFIGURATION
Flowing smoothly, unhurried

CHRISTOPHER DEARNLEY

1 Once___ on a moun-tain top there stood three start - led men who saw the veil of na - ture drop and hea-ven shine in. Their friend of ev' - ry day, the face they knew___ for his, they saw for one half - hour the way he al - - - ways is.

2 Yet___ men have lived and died and found of God___ no trace. 'Thou art a God' (the pro-phet cried) 'who hi-dest thy face.' The earth lies all ex - plored, the heavens are ours___ to climb; and___ still no man has seen his God at a - - - ny time.

3 And___ minds that learn to scan cre - a - tion like___ a book say no - thing lives out - side their plan, and so ne - ver look. O Lord of hid - den light, for-give us who___ des - pise the ___ things which lie be - yond our sight, and give us eyes.

1   Once on a mountain-top
there stood three startled men
who saw the veil of nature drop
    and heaven shine in.
Their friend of every day,
the face they knew for his,
they saw for one half-hour the way
    he always is.

2   Yet men have lived and died
and found of God no trace.
'Thou art a God' (the prophet cried)
    'who hidest thy face.'
The earth lies all explored,
the heavens are ours to climb;
and still no man has seen his God
    at any time.

3   And minds that learn to scan
creation like a book
say nothing lives outside their plan
    and so never look.
O Lord of hidden light,
forgive us who despise
the things which lie beyond our sight
    and give us eyes.

Michael Hewlett (b. 1916), *alta*

76

NAPHILL

HAROLD DARKE (b. 1888)

Our Lord, his pass-ion en - ded, hath glo-rious-ly as - cen - ded,

yet though from him di - vi - ded, he leaves us not un - gui - ded;

all his ben - e - fits to — crown he hath sent his Spi - rit down,

burn - ing like a flame of fire his dis - ci - ples to in-spire.

1 Our Lord, his passion ended,
hath gloriously ascended,
yet though from him divided,
he leaves us not unguided;
  all his benefits to crown
  he hath sent his Spirit down,
burning like a flame of fire
his disciples to inspire.

2 God's Spirit is directing;
no more they sit expecting;
but forth to all the nation
they go with exultation;
  that which God in them hath wrought
  fills their life and soul and thought,
so their witness now can do
work as great in others too.

3 The centuries go gliding
but still we have abiding
with us that Spirit Holy
to make us brave and lowly—
  lowly, for we feel our need,
  God alone is strong indeed;
brave, for with the Spirit's aid
we can venture unafraid.

4 O Lord of every nation,
fill us with inspiration!
We know our own unfitness,
yet for thee would bear witness.
  By thy Spirit now we raise
  to the heavenly Father praise:
Holy Spirit, Father, Son,
make us know thee, ever One.

F. C. Burkitt (1864–1935)

77

OSBORNE

HENRY CAREY (1692?–1743)
adapted and arranged by R. VAUGHAN WILLIAMS (1872–1958)

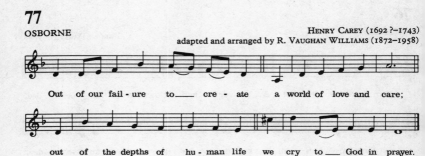

Out of our fail-ure to___ cre-ate a world of love and care;

out of the depths of hu-man life we cry to___ God in prayer.

Psalm 130

1 Out of our failure to create
 a world of love and care;
 out of the depths of human life
 we cry to God in prayer.

2 Out of the darkness of our time,
 of days for ever gone,
 our souls are longing for the light,
 like watchmen for the dawn.

3 Out of the depths we cry to him
 whose will is strong and just;
 all human hole-and-corner ways
 are by his light exposed.

4 Hope in the Lord whose timeless love
 gives laughter where we wept;
 the father, who at every point
 his word has given and kept.

Fred Kaan (b. 1929)

For verse 3 cf. *John* 3: 19–21.

BUNESSAN

Gaelic Melody

Praise and thanks-giv - ing, Fa - ther, we of - fer for all things
liv - ing thou mad - est good. Har-vest of sown fields, fruits of the
orch - ard, hay from the mown fields, blos - som and wood.

1 Praise and thanksgiving,
  Father, we offer
  for all things living
      thou madest good.
          Harvest of sown fields,
          fruits of the orchard,
          hay from the mown fields,
          blossom and wood.

2 Bless thou the labour
  we bring to serve thee,
  that with our neighbour
      we may be fed.
          Sowing or tilling
          we would work with thee;
          harvesting, milling,
          for daily bread.

3 Father, providing
  food for thy children,
  thy wisdom guiding
      teaches us share
          one with another,
          so that rejoicing
          with us, our brother
          may know thy care.

4 Then will thy blessing
  reach every people,
  all men confessing
      thy gracious hand.
          Where thy will reigneth
          no man will hunger,
          thy love sustaineth;
          fruitful the land.

Albert Frederick Bayly (b. 1901)

79

LAUDATE PUERI

HEINZ WERNER ZIMMERMANN, (b. 1930)

Praise the Lord! ___ Praise, you serv - ants of the Lord, ___ praise the

name of the Lord! _____ Blessèd ___ be the name of the Lord! ___

Blessèd ___ be the name of the Lord ___ from this time forth and for

e - ver - more! Praise the Lord! ___ Praise the Lord! ___

1 Praise the Lord!
  Praise, you servants of the Lord,
  praise the name of the Lord!
  Blessed be the name of the Lord!
  Blessed be the name of the Lord
  from this time forth and for evermore!
  Praise the Lord!
  Praise the Lord!

2 Praise the Lord!
  Thanks and praises sing to God,
  day by day to the Lord!
  High above the nations is God.
  High above the nations is God,
  his glory high over earth and sky.
  Praise the Lord!
  Praise the Lord!

3 Praise the Lord!
  Praise and glory give to God!
  Who is like unto him?
  Raising up the poor from the dust,
  raising up the poor from the dust,
  he makes them dwell in his heart and home.
  Praise the Lord!
  Praise the Lord!

4 Praise the Lord!
  Praise, you servants of the Lord,
  praise the love of the Lord!
  Giving to the homeless a home,
  giving to the homeless a home,
  he fills their hearts with new hope and joy.
  Praise the Lord!
  Praise the Lord!

Marjorie Jillson

80

ONE-FIFTY

FIRST TUNE

LAWRENCE BARTLETT (b. 1933)
Descant by JOHN WILSON

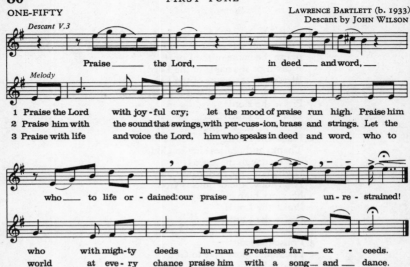

Praise the Lord, in deed and word,

Melody

1 Praise the Lord with joy-ful cry; let the mood of praise run high. Praise him
2 Praise him with the sound that swings, with per-cuss-ion, brass and strings. Let the
3 Praise with life and voice the Lord, him who speaks in deed and word, who to

who to life or-dained: our praise un-re-strained!

who with migh-ty deeds hu-man greatness far ex - ceeds.
world at eve-ry chance praise him with a song and dance.
life the world or - dained: let our praise be un - re - strained!

SECOND TUNE

ORIENTIS PARTIBUS

Mediaeval French melody
harmonised by Eric H. Thiman

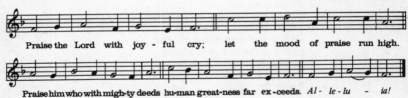

Praise the Lord with joy - ful cry; let the mood of praise run high.

Praise him who with migh-ty deeds hu-man great-ness far ex-ceeds. Al - le - lu - ia!

Psalm 150

1 Praise the Lord with joyful cry;
let the mood of praise run high.
Praise him who with mighty deeds
human greatness far exceeds.

2 Praise him with the sound that swings,
with percussion, brass and strings.
Let the world at every chance
praise him with a song and dance.

3 Praise with life and voice the Lord,
him who speaks in deed and word,
who to life the world ordained:
let our praise be unrestrained!

Fred Kaan (b. 1929)

When the second tune is used, *Alleluia* may be sung after each verse.

81

RASUMOVSKY

Russian melody, arranged by MARTIN SHAW (1875–1958)

All Sing: *Moderato e maestoso*

1. Praise to God — in the high - - est! Bless us, O
3. May the truth — in its beau - - ty flour - ish tri -
5. May the good — be o - beyed, — and e - vil be
7. Peace on earth, — and good - will. — be ev - er a -

Fa - ther!
umph - ant: *Praise ___ to ___ thee!*
con - quered:
mongst us:

Choir sing verses 2, 4 and 6.

1 Praise to God in the highest! Bless us, O Father!
   Praise to thee !

2 Guide and prosper the nations, rulers and people:

3 May the truth in its beauty flourish triumphant:

4 May the mills bring us bread, for food and for giving:

5 May the good be obeyed, and evil be conquered:

6 Give us laughter, and set us gaily rejoicing:

7 Peace on earth, and goodwill, be ever amongst us.
   Praise to thee !

Russian, tr. Percy Dearmer (1867–1936)

82

WORLEBURY

JOHN AINSLIE

Reap me the earth as a har-vest to God; gath-er and bring it a - gain,___

all that is his, to the Ma - ker of all: lift it and of - fer it

high!___ *Bring bread, bring wine, give glo — ry to the Lord.*

Whose is the earth but God's? Whose is the praise but his?

1 Reap me the earth as a harvest to God;
       gather and bring it again,
   all that is his, to the Maker of all:
       lift it and offer it high!
           Bring bread, bring wine, give glory to the Lord.
           Whose is the earth but God's?
           Whose is the praise but his?

2 Go with your song and your music, with joy
       go to the altar of God.
   Carry your offerings, fruits of the earth,
       work of your labouring hands.

3 Gladness and pity and passion and pain
       —all that is mortal in man—
   lay all before him, return him his gift—
       God, to whom all shall go home.

'Peter Icarus'

83

CHESHUNT

Fast

RICHARD H. JACQUET (b. 1947)

Ring a bell for peace, for the babe born on this night, ring a bell thro' the country and the town; ring a bell for peace, come and see the wondrous light, ring a bell, ring it merry up and down.

1 Ring a bell for peace,
    for the babe born on this night,
      ring a bell through the country and the town;
  ring a bell for peace,
    come and see the wondrous light,
      ring a bell, ring it merry up and down.

2 Blow a horn for joy,
    for the babe born in the hay,
      blow a horn through the country and the town;
  blow a horn for joy,
    come and hear what people say,
      blow a horn, blow it merry up and down.

3 Play a flute for hope,
    for the babe now fast asleep,
      play a flute through the country and the town;
  play a flute for hope,
    see the shepherds leave their sheep,
      play a flute, play it merry up and down.

4 Beat the drum for faith,
    for the babe born 'neath the star,
      beat the drum through the country and the town;
  beat the drum for faith,
    come and play where'er you are,
      beat the drum, beat it merry up and down.

Marian Collihole

84

SEE THE BABY (AMEN)

Negro Spiritual
arranged by Geoffrey Laycock

CONGREGATIONAL PART

A — men, a — — men, a — — men, a — men, a —

Solo or semichorus

1 See the ba - by ly - ing in a man - ger
2 See him in the tem - ple, teach - er of the teach - ers
3 See him at the sea - side heal - ing and pro - claim - ing
4 See him in the gar - den pray - ing to his Fa - ther
5 Yes, he is our Sa - viour. Je - sus died to save us,
6 Hal - le - lu - jah in the heav'n-ly King - dom

CONGREGATIONAL PART

men, a — men, a —

on that Christ - mas__ morn - ing.
marv'-lling at his__ wis - dom.
to the strong and__ fee - ble.
in the deep - est__ sor - row.
and he rose at__ Eas - ter.
with our li - ving__ Sa - viour!

men, a — men, a — men, a — men.

(Amen, amen, amen. . .)

1 See the baby
lying in a manger
on that Christmas morning.

2 See him in the temple
teacher of the teachers
marv'lling at his wisdom.

3 See him at the seaside
healing and proclaiming
to the strong and feeble.

4 See him in the garden
praying to his Father
in the deepest sorrow.

5 Yes, he is our Saviour.
Jesus died to save us,
and he rose at Easter.

6 Hallelujah
in the heav'nly Kingdom
with our living Saviour!
(. . . amen, amen.)

Traditional, altd.

85

BABEL

SVEN-ERIK BÄCK
in 71 *Psalmer och Visor,* 1971

See them build-ing Ba-bel's tower: slaves the stones are carr-ying. Here

no man cares for bro-ther man: Ky - ri-e - lei-son!

(Vv. 4-7) Hal - - le - lu - jah!

Babel

1 See them building Babel's tower:
    slaves the stones are carrying.
  Here no man cares for brother man.
    Kyrieleison!

2 Far astray that upward road.
    Man, become a stranger,
  goes hungry at his brother's board—
    Kyrieleison!

3 'Brotherhood'—forgotten word
    down the grassy hillside
  rejected from that building lies.
    Kyrieleison!

4 Men one day will find it there
    and will recognize it
  as keystone of God's hill and house.
    Hallelujah!

5 Then their cry will rise, and we
    each in his own language
  shall hear of brotherhood once more.
    Hallelujah!

6 Mighty wind of heaven's rule,
    storming every barrier,
  will blow for ever where it wills.
    Hallelujah!

7 So shall Babel come to nought:
    where it stood shall flourish
  the harvest of God's brotherhood.
    Hallelujah!

Olov Hartman,
tr. Caryl Micklem (b. 1925)
and Ruth Micklem (b. 1930)

86 THE BEATITUDES

Set to music by WILLIAM LLEWELLYN (b. 1925)

NOTE: *Each bar, whether $\frac{2}{4}$ or $\frac{3}{4}$ is to have the same duration.*

ANTIPHON (sung by ALL)

tain ___ mer - cy.   𝆑 Show us your ways, ___ O Lord, teach us your

paths. ___   Blest are the pure ___ in heart;   for they shall

Solo   *All (or Choir)*

see God.   Blest are ___ the peace-ma-kers;   for

Solo   *All (or Choir)*

they shall be called God's sons.   Blest are they which are per-se-cu-ted

Solo

for right-eous-ness' sake;   the king-dom of heav'n is theirs.

All (or Choir)

ANTIPHON (sung by ALL)

𝆑 Show us your ways, ___ O Lord, teach us your paths. ___

Words from Psalm 25, v. 4
and Matthew 5, vv. 3-10

87

DAVID MCCARTHY (b. 1931)

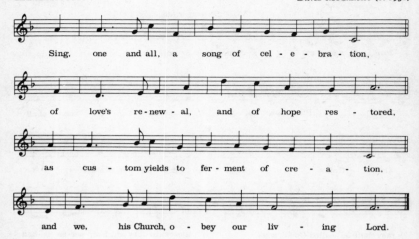

Sing, one and all, a song of cel-e-bra-tion,

of love's re-new-al, and of hope res-tored,

as cus-tom yields to fer-ment of cre-a-tion,

and we, his Church, o-bey our liv-ing Lord.

A song of celebration

1 Sing, one and all, a song of celebration,
   of love's renewal, and of hope restored,
   as custom yields to ferment of creation,
   and we, his Church, obey our living Lord.

2 Rejoice that still his Spirit is descending
   with challenges that faith cannot refuse;
   and ask no longer what is worth defending,
   but how to make effective God's good news.

3 We need not now take refuge in tradition,
   like men prepared to make a final stand,
   but use it as a springboard of decision,
   to follow him whose Kingdom is at hand—

4 to follow him: to share his way of living;
   to shape the future as, in him, we should;
   to step across the frontiers of forgiving,
   and bear the burdens of true brotherhood.

5 Creative Spirit, let your word be spoken!
   Your shock of truth invigorates the mind;
   your miracles of grace shall be our token
   that only God in Christ can save mankind.

F. Pratt Green (b. 1903)

88

GOFFS OAK

RICHARD H. JACQUET (b. 1947)

Sing to the Lord, _____ stars and beau-ti-ful sun, mill-ions of rain-drops, sing!

Brooks and ri-vers that run, _____ sing to the Lord!

1 Sing to the Lord,
  stars and beautiful sun,
  millions of raindrops, sing!
  Brooks and rivers that run,
  sing to the Lord!

2 Sing to the Lord,
  rolling waves on the sand,
  seaweed and pebbles, sing!
  Mighty mountains that stand,
  sing to the Lord!

3 Sing to the Lord,
  wheat that sways in the breeze,
  ants ever busy, sing!
  Cheerful birds in the trees,
  sing to the Lord!

4 Sing to the Lord,
  playful kittens and lambs,
  mothers and children, sing!
  Smiling babies in prams,
  sing to the Lord!

5 Sing to the Lord,
  great and wonderful world,
  children and grown-ups, sing!
  Songs of praise for this world
  sing to the Lord!

Marie Odile Herve

89

STEIN

ROLF SCHWEIZER

REFRAIN

Sing to the Lord a new song, for he does won-ders.

Sing to the Lord a new song, for he does won-ders.

1 God
2 You
3 —
4 You

Last time   Fine

won - ders.

1 tri - umphs __ for he is right - eous,
2 think God __ is the Un - known One,
3 Of - ten you don't know his pur - pose,
4 must learn __ to see him on - ly

and his sa - cred - ness is his strength: the Lord has de-clared his
that his power is of small ac - count? that God can't see what op-
or what is the right thing to do, but God sends his help to
as the Fa - ther who guides your life: this ve - ry day he holds

D.C.

sav-ing power; he ev'-ry-where dis - plays his righteousness. _____
pres-ses you? Look at your life, how he takes care of it! _____
ev'-ry-one who tru - ly seeks to un - der - stand his will. _____
out his hand; so seize it now and do not turn a - way. _____

God's caring power

REFRAIN

    Sing to the Lord a new song, for he does wonders.
    Sing to the Lord a new song, for he does wonders.

1 God triumphs for he is righteous,
    and his sacredness is his strength:
    the Lord has declared his saving power;
    he everywhere displays his righteousness.
      Sing to the Lord. . .

2 You think God is the Unknown One,
    that his power is of small account?
    that God can't see what oppresses you?
    Look at your life, how he takes care of it!
      Sing to the Lord. . .

3 Often you don't know his purpose,
    or what is the right thing to do,
    but God sends his help to everyone
    who truly seeks to understand his will.
      Sing to the Lord. . .

4 You must learn to see him only
    as the Father who guides your life:
    this very day he holds out his hand;
    so seize it now and do not turn away.
      Sing to the Lord. . .

Paulus Stein
tr. F. Pratt Green (b. 1903)

An optional instrumental introduction is provided in the Full Music Edition.

90
PATTERNS

YVONNE GOODING
and compilers

Skip-ping down the pave-ment wide, count the pav - ing stones;

big or small or square or round, see their pat - terns on the ground.

House and fac - tory, church and shop, bricks and stones reach high.

Bus - y work-men made them all: see their pat - terns on the wall.

Patterns

1 Skipping down the pavement wide,
    count the paving stones;
  big or small or square or round,
    see their patterns on the ground.
  House and factory, church and shop,
    bricks and stones reach high.
  Busy workmen made them all:
    see their patterns on the wall.

2 Look above the rooftops tall,
    far as you can see.
  Clouds in daytime; stars at night;
    see their patterns in the sky.
  People walking down the street,
    dressed in colours gay;
  stripes and circles, frills and bows:
    see the patterns in their clothes.

3 Clouds and sunshine, night-time stars,
    clothes and curtains too;
  stones and pavement, bricks and wall:
    see the patterns in them all.
  Thank you, God, for sights to see
    round us every day:
  still or moving; big or small;
    and the patterns in them all!

Donald H. Hilton (b. 1932)

91

ASKERSWELL

PETER CUTTS (b. 1937)

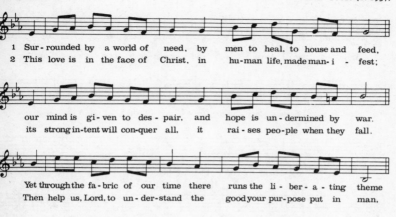

1 Sur-rounded by a world of need, by men to heal, to house and feed,
2 This love is in the face of Christ, in hu-man life, made man-i-fest;

our mind is gi-ven to des-pair, and hope is un-dermined by war.
its strong in-tent will con-quer all, it rai-ses peo-ple when they fall.

Yet through the fa-bric of our time there runs the li-ber-a-ting theme
Then help us, Lord, to un-der-stand the good your pur-pose put in man,

of love that makes the world go round, of love cre-a-tive and pro-found.
and use, to bring your reign a-bout, those in the church and those with-out.

Creative love

1 Surrounded by a world of need,
   by men to heal, to house and feed,
   our mind is given to despair,
   and hope is undermined by war.
   Yet through the fabric of our time
   there runs the liberating theme
   of love that makes the world go round,
   of love creative and profound.

2 This love is in the face of Christ,
   in human life, made manifest;
   its strong intent will conquer all,
   it raises people when they fall.
   Then help us, Lord, to understand
   the good your purpose put in man,
   and use, to bring your reign about,
   those in the church and those without.

Fred Kaan (b. 1929)

92

WINTON

GEORGE DYSON, (1883–196

Tell out, my soul, the great-ness of the Lord!

Un - num - bered bless - ings, give my spi - rit voice;

ten - der to me the pro - mise of his word;

in God my Sa - viour shall my heart re - joice.

Magnificat

1 Tell out, my soul, the greatness of the Lord!
      Unnumbered blessings, give my spirit voice;
   tender to me the promise of his word;
      in God my Saviour shall my heart rejoice.

2 Tell out, my soul, the greatness of his name!
      Make known his might, the deeds his arm has done;
   his mercy sure, from age to age the same;
      his holy name—the Lord, the Mighty One.

3 Tell out, my soul, the greatness of his might!
      Powers and dominions lay their glory by;
   proud hearts and stubborn wills are put to flight,
      the hungry fed, the humble lifted high.

4 Tell out, my soul, the glories of his word!
      Firm is his promise, and his mercy sure.
   Tell out, my soul, the greatness of the Lord
      to children's children and for evermore!

Timothy Dudley-Smith (b. 1926)

93

DEANE

CARYL MICKLEM (b. 1925)

Thank you, Lord, for wa-ter, soil and air — large gifts sup-port-ing

ev-ery-thing that lives. For-give our spoil-ing and a-buse of them.

Help us re-new the face of the earth.

HOLNICOTE   SECOND TUNE   CHARLES EDWARD STRANGE

Thank you, Lord, for wa-ter, soil and air — large gifts sup-port-ing

eve-ry-thing that lives. For-give our spoil-ing and a-buse of them.

Vv. 1-4   *V.5*

Help us re-new the face of the earth. Come ___ and re-new the face of the earth.

Caring for planet Earth

1 Thank you, Lord, for water, soil and air—
   large gifts supporting everything that lives.
      Forgive our spoiling and abuse of them.
      Help us renew the face of the earth.

2 Thank you, Lord, for minerals and ores—
   the basis of all building, wealth and speed.
      Forgive our reckless plundering and waste.
      Help us renew the face of the earth.

3 Thank you, Lord, for priceless energy—
   stored in each atom, gathered from the sun.
      Forgive our greed and carelessness of power.
      Help us renew the face of the earth.

4 Thank you, Lord, for weaving nature's life
   into a seamless robe, a fragile whole.
      Forgive our haste, that tampers unawares.
      Help us renew the face of the earth.

5 Thank you, Lord, for making planet Earth
   a home for us and ages yet unborn.
      Help us to share, consider, save and store.
      Come and renew the face of the earth.

Brian Wren (b. 1936)

94

GREEN LAKE

ERIK ROUTLEY (b. 1917

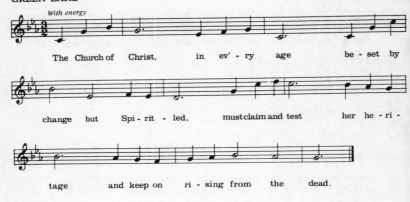

The Church of Christ, in ev'-ry age be-set by change but Spi-rit-led, must claim and test her he-ri-tage and keep on ri-sing from the dead.

The caring Church

1 The Church of Christ, in every age
    beset by change but Spirit-led,
    must claim and test her heritage
    and keep on rising from the dead.

2 She has no mission but to serve,
    in proud obedience to her Lord;
    to care for all, without reserve,
    to spread his liberating word.

3 Across a world, across the street,
    the victims of injustice cry
    for shelter and for bread to eat,
    and never live before they die.

4 And all men suffer deeper ills:
    for there's a fever in our blood
    that prostitutes our human skills
    and poisons all our brotherhood.

5 Then let the Servant Church arise,
    a caring Church that longs to be
    a partner in Christ's sacrifice,
    and clothed in Christ's humanity.

6 For he alone, whose blood was shed,
    can cure the fever in our blood,
    and teach us how to share our bread
    and feed the starving multitude.

F. Pratt Green (b. 1903)

95

KING'S LANGLEY

Traditional May-Day carol melody, collected
by Lucy Broadwood (1858–1929) and
harmonised by R. Vaughan Williams (1872–1958)

1,2 & 3. The glo-ry of our King was seen
1 when he came ri-ding by, ___
2 when, with his arms stretched wide ___
3 on the first Eas-ter day, ___

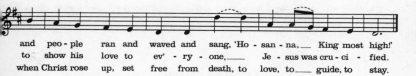

and peo-ple ran and waved and sang, 'Ho-san-na, ___ King most high!'
to show his love to ev'-ry-one, ___ Je-sus was cru-ci-fied.
when Christ rose up, set free from death, to love, to ___ guide, to stay.

1 The glory of our King was seen
   when he came riding by,
  and people ran and waved and sang
   'Hosanna, King most high!'

2 The glory of our King was seen
   when, with his arms stretched wide
  to show his love to everyone,
   Jesus was crucified.

3 The glory of our King was seen
   on the first Easter day,
  when Christ rose up, set free from death,
   to love, to guide, to stay.

Margaret Cropper, altd.

96

ST ETHELWALD

W. H. MONK (1823–89)

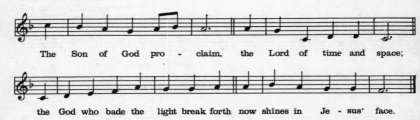

The Son of God pro - claim, the Lord of time and space;

the God who bade the light break forth now shines in Je - sus' face.

Lord of life and death

1 The Son of God proclaim,
    the Lord of time and space;
  the God who bade the light break forth
    now shines in Jesus' face.

2 He, God's creative Word,
    the Church's Lord and Head,
  here bids us gather as his friends
    and share his wine and bread.

3 The Lord of life and death
    with wondering praise we sing;
  we break the bread at his command
    and name him God and King.

4 We take this cup in hope;
    for he, who gladly bore
  the shameful cross, is risen again
    and reigns for evermore.

Basil E. Bridge (b. 1927)

BLACKBIRD LEYS

PETER CUTTS (b. 1937)

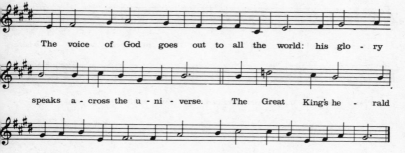

The voice of God goes out to all the world: his glo - ry

speaks a - cross the u - ni - verse. The Great King's he - rald

cries from star to star: *with power, with jus - tice, he will walk his way.*

Christ, the healing Word of God

1 The voice of God goes out to all the world:
his glory speaks across the universe.
The Great King's herald cries from star to star:
with power, with justice, he will walk his way.

2 The Lord has said: 'Receive my messenger,
my promise to the world, my pledge made flesh,
a lamp to every nation, light from light:
with power, with justice, he will walk his way'.

3 The broken reed he will not trample down,
nor set his heel upon the dying flame.
He binds the wounds, and health is in his hand:
with power, with justice, he will walk his way.

4 Anointed with the Spirit and with power,
he comes to crown with comfort all the weak,
to show the face of justice to the poor:
with power, with justice, he will walk his way.

5 His touch will bless the eyes that darkness held,
the lame shall run, the halting tongue shall sing,
and prisoners laugh in light and liberty:
with power, with justice, he will walk his way.

'Peter Icarus'

LAUDS

JOHN WILSON (b. 1905)

There's a spi - rit in the air, tel - ling Chris - tians ev - ery-where:

'Praise the love that Christ re-vealed, liv - ing, work-ing, in our world.'

OPTIONAL DESCANT FOR VERSES 4 & 7

Sopranos. (Other voices sing unison melody).

Praise___ the love!___ Praise___ the love!___

Al – – – le - lu - ia! Al – – – le - lu - ia!

'Praise the Holy Spirit'

1 There's a spirit in the air,
   telling Christians everywhere:
      'Praise the love that Christ revealed,
      living, working, in our world'.

      2 Lose your shyness, find your tongue,
         tell the world what God has done:
            God in Christ has come to stay.
            We can see his power today.

3 When believers break the bread,
   when a hungry child is fed,
      praise the love that Christ revealed,
      living, working, in our world.

      4 Still his Spirit leads the fight,
         seeing wrong and setting right:
            God in Christ has come to stay.
            We can see his power today.

5 When a stranger's not alone,
   where the homeless find a home,
      praise the love that Christ revealed,
      living, working, in our world.

      6 May his Spirit fill our praise,
         guide our thoughts and change our ways.
            God in Christ has come to stay.
            We can see his power today.

7 There's a Spirit in the air,
   calling people everywhere:
      praise the love that Christ revealed,
      living, working, in our world.

Brian Wren (b. 1936)

99

GAUDIUM ET SPES

BRIAN WREN (b. 1936)
and compilers

This we can do   for jus-tice and for peace: we can pray, and work to an-swer

prayers that oth - er peo- ple say. This we can do in   faith   and see it

through —   for Je - sus is a - live to - day.   (2) This we can

This we can do

1 This we can do for justice and for peace:
        we can pray,
    and work to answer prayers that other people say.
    This we can do in faith
    and see it through—
        for Jesus is alive today.

2 This we can do for justice and for peace:
        we can give
    till every man can take life in his hands, and live.
    This we can do in love
    and see it through—
        for Jesus is alive today.

3 This we can do for justice and for peace:
        we can see—
    and help our neighbours see—what is, and what could be.
    This we can do with truth
    and see it through—
        for Jesus is alive today.

4 This we can do for justice and for peace:
        we can fight
    whatever hurts and tramples down, or hides the light.
    This we can do with strength
    and see it through—
        for Jesus is alive today.

5 This we can do for justice and for peace:
        we can hope
    and, hoping, stride along our way while others grope.
    This we can do till God
    makes all things new—
        for Jesus is alive today.

TROTTING   ERIC REID (1936–1970)

Trot - ting, trot - ting through Je - ru - sa - lem,
Je - sus, sit - ting on a __ don - key's back, chil - dren wav - ing
bran - ches, sing - ing 'Hap - py is he that __ comes in the name of the
Lord!' __

Palm Sunday

1   Trotting, trotting through Jerusalem,
     Jesus, sitting on a donkey's back,
     children waving branches, singing
     'Happy is he that comes in the name of the Lord!'

2   Many people in Jerusalem
     thought he should have come on a mighty horse
     leading all the Jews to battle—
     'Happy is he that comes in the name of the Lord!'

3   Many people in Jerusalem
     were amazed to see such a quiet man
     trotting, trotting on a donkey—
     'Happy is he that comes in the name of the Lord!'

4   Trotting, trotting through Jerusalem,
     Jesus, sitting on a donkey's back:
     let us join the children singing
     'Happy is he that comes in the name of the Lord!'

Eric Reid (1934–1970)

101

MALHAM

PETER CUTTS (b. 1937)

1 Un - der the ar - ches of the night mo - thers are
2 Un - der the sky - light of a star Ma - ry re -
3 So may we all take heart and sing praise to the

sing - ing lull - a - bies and fill with won - der
gards her lit - tle son; pre - cious to her as
light of life on earth, lull - a - by to the

at the sight of glo - ry shut in sleep - ing
gift from far this mar - vel of a life___ be -
in - fant king who's born to bless all hu - man

Descant for V.3

birth, put - ting all grief and fear to

Unison melody

eyes. In - ti - mate stran - ger seems to
gun, while in God's fu - ture lies un -
birth, put - ting all grief and fear to

flight be - neath the ar - ches of ___ the night.

be the child u - pon a mo - ther's knee.
known the sec - ret of that life___ laid down.
flight be - neath the ar - ches of ___ the night.

Under the arches of the night

1 Under the arches of the night
    mothers are singing lullabies
  and fill with wonder at the sight
    of glory shut in sleeping eyes.
        Intimate stranger seems to be
        the child upon a mother's knee.

2 Under the skylight of a star
    Mary regards her little son:
  precious to her as gift from far
    this marvel of a life begun,
        while in God's future lies unknown
        the secret of that life laid down.

3 So may we all take heart and sing
    praise to the Light of life on earth,
  lullaby to the infant King
    who's born to bless all human birth,
        putting all grief and fear to flight
        beneath the arches of the night.

Caryl Micklem (b. 1925)

102
FIFEHEAD

CARYL MICKLEM (b. 192?)

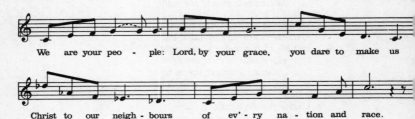

We are your peo - ple: Lord, by your grace, you dare to make us

Christ to our neigh - bours of ev' - ry na - tion and race.

The Church taking stock of itself

1 We are your people:
  Lord, by your grace,
      you dare to make us
      Christ to our neighbours
  of every nation and race.

2 How can we demonstrate
  your love and care—
      speaking or listening?
      battling or serving?
  help us to know when and where.

3 Called to portray you,
  help us to live
      closer than neighbours
      open to strangers,
  able to clash and forgive.

4 Glad of tradition,
  help us to see
      in all life's changing
      where you are leading,
  where our best efforts should be.

5 Joined in community,
  breaking your bread,
      may we discover
      gifts in each other,
  willing to lead and be led.

6 Lord, as we minister
  in different ways,
      may all we're doing
      show that you're living,
  meeting your love with our praise.

Brian Wren (b. 1936)

INTERCESSOR   C. HUBERT H. PARRY (1848–1918)

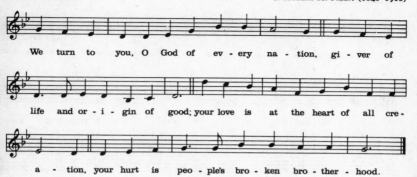

The family of nations

1 We turn to you, O God of every nation,
   giver of life and origin of good;
   your love is at the heart of all creation,
   your hurt is people's broken brotherhood.

2 We turn to you that we may be forgiven
   for crucifying Christ on earth again.
   We know that we have never wholly striven,
   forgetting self, to love the other man.

3 Free every heart from pride and self-reliance,
   our ways of thought inspire with simple grace;
   break down among us barriers of defiance,
   speak to the soul of all the human race.

4 Teach us, good Lord, to serve the need of others,
   help us to give and not to count the cost.
   Unite us all for we are born as brothers;
   defeat our Babel with your Pentecost.

Fred Kaan (b. 1929)

104

PHILIPPIAN

CARYL MICKLEM (b. 1925)

We praise you, Lord, for all that's true and pure —— clean lines, clear water, and an hon-est mind. Grant us your truth, keep guard ov-er our hearts, fill all our thoughts with these things.

Philippians 4.6–8

1 We praise you, Lord, for all that's true and pure—
clean lines, clear water, and an honest mind.
Grant us your truth, keep guard over our hearts,
fill all our thoughts with these things.

2 We praise you, Lord, for all that's excellent—
high mountain peaks, achievement dearly won.
Lift up our eyes, keep guard over our hearts,
fill all our thoughts with these things.

3 We praise you, Lord, for all of good report—
the spur to us of others' noble lives.
Show us your will, keep guard over our hearts,
fill all our thoughts with these things.

4 We praise you, Lord, the man of Nazareth—
you lived for others, now you live for all.
Jesus, draw near, keep guard over our hearts,
fill all our thoughts with these things.

Caryl Micklem (b. 1925)

Traditional Irish tune
arranged by compilers

1 When I see the sal-mon leap the fall, or the aer'-plane's sil-ver trail — or a
3 When I breathe the smell of clean fresh air blowing soft - ly af-ter rain; — when the

drop of wa-ter mag-ni-fied, then my eyes and heart bless the Lord. 2 When I
strawberries are turned to jam, then my nose and heart bless the Lord. 4 At the

hear the fros-ty crunch of snow, or the sun-drenched hum —— of the bee, —— or a
taste of ber-ries gathered free, or the tang of sea-food, mint or trea-cle,touch of

well-tuned en-gine whine with pow'r, then my ears and heart bless the Lord.
vel - vet, feel of cold smooth stones, hands and tongue and heart bless the Lord.

Praise with every sense

1 When I see the salmon leap the fall,
   or the aer'plane's silver trail—
   or a drop of water magnified,
   then my eyes and heart bless the Lord.

2 When I hear the frosty crunch of snow,
   or the sun-drenched hum of the bee,
   or a well-tuned engine whine with power,
   then my ears and heart bless the Lord.

3 When I breathe the smell of clean fresh air
   blowing softly after rain,
   when the strawberries are turned to jam,
   then my nose and heart bless the Lord.

4 At the taste of berries gathered free,
   or the tang of sea-food, mint or treacle,
   touch of velvet, feel of cold smooth stones,
   hands and tongue and heart bless the Lord.

Gracie King, altd.

106

C. V. STANFORD (1852–1924)

When, in man's mu - sic, God is glo - ri - fied, _____
and a - dor - a - tion leaves no room for pride, _____ it is as
though the whole cre - a - tion cried: _____ Al - - le - lu - ia!

A - - men.

For a festival of praise

1 When, in man's music, God is glorified,
   and adoration leaves no room for pride,
   it is as though the whole creation cried
       Alleluia !

2 How oft, in making music, we have found
   a new dimension in the world of sound,
   as worship moved us to a more profound
       Alleluia !

3 So has the Church, in liturgy and song,
   in faith and love, through centuries of wrong,
   borne witness to the truth in every tongue.
       Alleluia !

4 And did not Jesus sing a psalm that night
   when utmost evil strove against the Light ?
   then let us sing, for whom he won the fight,
       Alleluia !

5 Let every instrument be tuned for praise!
   Let all rejoice who have a voice to raise!
   And may God give us faith to sing always
       Alleluia ! Amen.

F. Pratt Green (b. 1903)

107

DAVID GOODALL (b. 1922)

When you start-ed off the un - i - verse, Lord most high,
_____ did you know just what would hap - pen as
years went by? _____ Did you in your
in - fin - ite mind ev' - ry - thing fore- see?_____ Or___ does
be - ing God ___ mean you make a place ___ for un -
cer - tain - ty? _____

1 When you started off the universe, Lord most high,
did you know just what would happen as years went by?
Did you in your infinite mind
everything foresee?
Or does being God mean you make a place for uncertainty?

2 When your Son allowed himself to be led away,
did he know you'd resurrect him on Easter Day?
Could he, there on Calvary's hill,
know what was to be?
Or did being yours mean he had to suffer uncertainty?

3 When your Spirit helps us all to be more complete,
seeking our co-operation and not defeat,
is it simply done for effect,
so that we'll feel free?
Or does being Spirit mean he can cope with uncertainty?

4 When we're told our faith has got to be more assured,
does it mean we ought to know all the answers, Lord?
If we had true faith in our God,
would our doubts all flee?
Or does having faith mean we thank you, Lord, for uncertainty?

John Gregory (b. 1929)

PETER CUTTS, (b. 1937)

Where is God to-day? Shall we find him wait-ing when we come to pray? Will he come a-gain ev'-ry Sun-day morn-ing? Do we wait in vain?

Interlude

1 Where is God today?
  Shall we find him waiting
  when we come to pray?
  Will he come again
  every Sunday morning?
  Do we wait in vain?

2 Or can two or three,
  four or five, or sixty
  in his name agree,
  so that we declare,
  'He is here among us,
  all our life to share'?

3 We have seen and heard
  that which we believe in;
  take him at his word.
  We have seen the face
  of eternal goodness,
  full of truth and grace.

4 God whose face we seek
  comes to life in Jesus
  seventy times a week.
  Every day he shows
  something of his glory
  to the man who knows.

5 This is how we know
  that we really see him—
  when like him we grow;
  gain for him was loss;
  for he lived for others
  till he gained the cross.

6 Now the feast displays
  all that he enacted;
  celebrates his praise.
  So once more we meet
  Death and Resurrection,
  and we stay—to eat.

David Goodall (b. 1922)

109

ILLSLEY

Melody, and most of the harmony,
by J. BISHOP (1665–1737)

Your light, O God, was given to man, the light of truth, your wis-dom's flame:

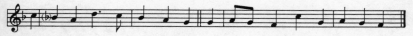

from age to age it grew more clear, and glor - ious shone when Je - sus came.

1 Your light, O God, was given to man,
    the light of truth, your wisdom's flame:
  from age to age it grew more clear,
    and glorious shone when Jesus came.

2 The light of all the world was he;
    but men loved darkness more than light.
  With evil deeds of pride and hate
    they scorned God's love and chose the night.

3 But light unconquered shone again;
    no cross or tomb its power could bind;
  in glory, love and life arose
    to shine for ever on mankind.

4 Forgive us, Lord, if we have spurned
    your truth, your light, your wisdom's way;
  and lead our hearts through Christ to find
    in love the road to perfect day.

Albert Frederick Bayly (b. 1901), *altd.*

110 GLORIA IN EXCELSIS

ERIK ROUTLEY (b. 1917)

Glo-ry to God in the highest, ____ and peace to his peo-ple on earth. ____ Lord God, hea-ven-ly King, ____ al - migh - ty God ____ and Fa - ther, ____ we wor-ship you, we give ____ you thanks, we praise you for ____ your glo-ry. ____ Lord Je-sus Christ, on - ly Son of the Father. ____ Lord God, ____ Lamb of God, ____ you take a - way the sin of the world: ____ have mercy up-on us; you are sea-ted at the right ____ hand of the Fa - ther: ____ re-ceive our prayer. For you a-lone are the Ho-ly one. ____ you a - lone are the Lord, ____ you a - lone are the Most High, Je - sus Christ, ____ with the Ho-ly Spi - rit in the glo - - ry of God ____ the Fa-ther. A - men!

111

SANCTUS AND BENEDICTUS

ERIK ROUTLEY (b. 1917)

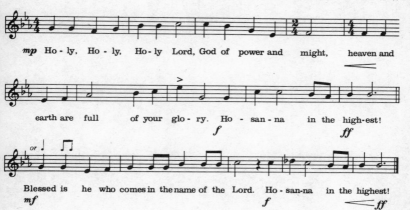

mp Ho-ly, Ho-ly, Ho-ly Lord, God of power and might, heaven and

earth are full of your glo-ry. Ho-san-na in the high-est!

Blessed is he who comes in the name of the Lord. Ho-san-na in the highest!

112

ACCLAMATIONS

ERIK ROUTLEY (b. 1917)

Maestoso

Christ has died. Christ is ris-en. In Christ shall

all be made a-live. Bles-sing and ho-nour and glo-ry and

power be to our God for e-ver and e-ver!

ORDER OF WORSHIP
FOR
THE LORD'S SUPPER

ACKNOWLEDGEMENTS

The publishers are grateful for permission to use material as indicated below:

The text of the Authorised Version of the Bible is Crown copyright and the extract used herein is reproduced by permission.

New English Bible, second edition copyright 1970 by permission of Oxford and Cambridge University Presses.

Verses from the *Revised Standard Version of the Bible*, copyrighted 1946 and 1952 by the Division of Christian Education of the National Council of the Churches of Christ in the USA.

Texts prepared by the International Consultation on English Texts (Texts of Gloria in Excelsis, Sursum Corda, Sanctus and Benedictus) published in *Prayers we have in common* (Geoffrey Chapman 1971).

The Lord's Prayer based on the version prepared by the International Consultation on English Texts, revised and printed in Series 3 Order for Holy Communion.

The paragraph 'We thank you that Jesus was born' from *Contemporary Prayers for Public Worship*, edited by Caryl Micklem, published by SCM Press Ltd.

ORDER OF WORSHIP
FOR THE LORD'S SUPPER

THE WORD AND THE PRAYERS

The Bible may be brought into the church, all standing; and the minister enters and may call the people to worship saying,

Let us worship God.

Scripture Sentences   (*all standing*)

Minister	This is the day which the Lord has made;
People	**let us rejoice and be glad in it.**
Minister	It is good to give thanks to the Lord;
People	**for his love endures for ever.**

Other sentences may be used or seasonal sentences added.

Prayer of Approach

Minister   Let us pray.

Almighty God,
to whom all hearts are open,
all desires known,
and from whom no secrets are hid:
cleanse the thoughts of our hearts
by the inspiration of your Holy Spirit,
that we may perfectly love you,
and worthily magnify your holy Name;
through Christ our Lord.   **Amen.**

Or this prayer may be used:

Almighty God, infinite and eternal
in wisdom, power and love:
we praise you for all that you are,
and for all that you do for the world.
You have shown us your truth and your love
in our Saviour Jesus Christ.
Help us by your Spirit
to worship you in spirit and in truth;
through Jesus Christ our Lord.   **Amen.**

Hymn or Psalm

Confession of Sin   (*all kneel or sit*)

Minister   Let us confess our sins to God
and ask his forgiveness.

| All | Lord God most merciful,
we confess that we have sinned,
through our own fault,
and in common with others,
in thought, word and deed,
and through what we have left undone. |
|---|---|

We ask to be forgiven.

By the power of your Spirit
turn us from evil to good,
help us to forgive others,
and keep us in your ways
of righteousness and love;
through Jesus Christ our Lord.   Amen.

Assurance of Pardon

| Minister | In repentance and in faith
receive the promise of grace
and the assurance of pardon: |
|---|---|

Here are words you may trust,
words that merit full acceptance:
'Christ Jesus came into the world to save sinners.'
Your sins are forgiven for his sake.

People	**Thanks be to God.**

Or this Assurance may be used:

| Minister | God so loved the world
that he gave his only Son,
that whoever believes in him
should not perish
but have eternal life. |
|---|---|

To all who repent and believe,
we declare, in the name of the Father,
the Son and the Holy Spirit:
God grants you
the forgiveness of your sins.

People	**Thanks be to God.**

The Kyries   *(may be said)*

Minister	Lord, have mercy on us.
People	**Christ, have mercy on us.**
Lord, have mercy on us.

Gloria in excelsis *(all standing)*

All   Glory to God in the highest,
      and peace to his people on earth.

      Lord God, heavenly King,
      almighty God and Father,
      we worship you, we give you thanks,
      we praise you for your glory.

      Lord Jesus Christ, only Son of the Father,
      Lord God, Lamb of God,
      you take away the sin of the world:
      have mercy on us;
      you are seated at the right hand of the Father:
      receive our prayer.

      For you alone are the Holy One,
      you alone are the Lord,
      you alone are the Most High,
      Jesus Christ, with the Holy Spirit,
      in the glory of God the Father. Amen.

Prayer for Grace

> *The collect of the day or other prayer for grace may be
> said here or after the sermon.*

*The Minister may then introduce the theme of the day's service, and may
speak in particular to the children, and a hymn may be sung before the children
leave; or the minister may speak to the children after one of the readings.*

Old Testament Reading

and/or a New Testament Reading

Psalm, Canticle, Hymn or Anthem

New Testament Reading

or readings: Epistle and Gospel

> *A hymn may be sung.*

Sermon

> *The sermon may be followed by a silence and/or a prayer.*

Hymn

> *The notices may be given here or after the prayers.*

Prayers for the Church and the World

After each paragraph a versicle and response may be said, such as

V.   Lord, in your mercy,
R.   Hear our prayer.

> *The special subjects after the words 'We pray for' are merely suggestions; others may be substituted; omissions may be made. Intervals of silence should be kept.*
> *The paragraphs may be used as a continuous prayer by the omission of the words 'We pray for' and the words in italics.*

Minister   Let us pray.

Almighty God,
whose Spirit helps us in our weakness
and guides us in our prayers;
we pray for the Church and for the world
in the name of Jesus Christ.

We pray for

the Church throughout the world
our ministers, elders and members
local unity and witness

Renew the faith and life of the Church;
strengthen its witness;
and make it one in Christ.
Grant that we
and all who confess that he is Lord
may be faithful in service
and filled with his spirit,
and that the world may be turned to him.

We pray for

the nations of the world
our own country
all who work for reconciliation

Guide the nations
in the ways of justice, liberty and peace;
and help them to seek
the unity and welfare of mankind.
Give to our Queen and to all in authority
wisdom to know and strength to do
what is right.

We pray for

those in trade and industry
members of the professions
all who serve the community

Grant that men and women in their various callings
may have grace to do their work well;
and may the resources of the earth be wisely used,
truth honoured and preserved,
and the quality of our life enriched.

We pray for

the sick and the suffering
victims of injustice
the lonely and the bereaved

Comfort those in sorrow;
heal the sick in body or in mind;
and deliver the oppressed.
Give us active sympathy
for all who suffer; and help us
so to bear the burdens of others
that we may fulfil the law of Christ.

We pray for

our families
friends and neighbours
all who need our prayers

Keep us and the members of our families
united in loyalty and in love,
and always in your care;
and may our friends and neighbours,
and all for whom we pray,
receive the help they need,
and live in peace.

We remember those who have died

Eternal God, accept our thanks and praise
for all who have served you faithfully here on earth,
and especially for those dear to our own hearts . . .
May we and all your people,
past, present and to come,
share the life and joy of your kingdom;
through Jesus Christ our Lord.   **Amen.**

The notices, if not already given, may be given here.

THE THANKSGIVING AND THE COMMUNION

The Invitation and the Gracious Words

The minister may then give an invitation to those present, to whatever branch of the Church they belong, to share in the Lord's Supper.

Minister	Hear the gracious words of our Lord Jesus Christ;

Come to me,
all who labour and are heavy-laden,
and I will give you rest.

I am the bread of life;
he who comes to me shall not hunger,
and he who believes in me shall never thirst.

Him who comes to me
I will not cast out.

The Peace

Minister	The peace of the Lord Jesus Christ be with you all.
People	**Peace be with you.**

Offertory

The offerings of the people are collected.

All stand when the offerings are brought to the Table.

The bread and wine may be carried into the church and brought to the Table; or, if they have been prepared on the Table before the service begins, the bread and wine are uncovered.

Then a prayer is said, all standing.

Minister	Let us pray.
All	**Eternal God, we come with these gifts to offer our sacrifice of praise and the service of our lives; through Jesus Christ our Lord. Amen.**

Hymn

This hymn may be sung while the money, bread and wine are brought to the Table, in which case the offertory prayer follows the hymn.

The Narrative of the Institution of the Lord's Supper (1 Corinthians 11: 23-26)

Minister   Hear the narrative of the institution
of the Lord's Supper as it was recorded
by the apostle Paul.

I received from the Lord what I also delivered
to you, that the Lord Jesus
on the night when he was betrayed
took bread, and when he had given thanks,
he broke it, and said,
'This is my body which is for you.
Do this in remembrance of me.'
In the same way also
the cup, after supper, saying,
'This cup is the new covenant in my blood.
Do this, as often as you drink it,
in remembrance of me.'
For as often as you eat this bread
and drink the cup, you proclaim the Lord's death
until he comes.

The Taking of the Bread and Wine

Minister   In the name of the Lord Jesus Christ,
and following his example,
we take this bread and this cup,
and give thanks to God.

The Thanksgiving   *(all standing)*

Minister   Lift up your hearts.
People   **We lift them to the Lord.**
Minister   Let us give thanks to the Lord our God.
People   **It is right to give him thanks and praise.**
Minister   With joy we give you thanks and praise,
Almighty God, Source of all life and love,
that we live in your world,
that you are always
creating and sustaining it by your power,
and that you have so made us
that we can know and love you,
trust and serve you.

We give you thanks
that you loved the world so much
that you gave your only Son,
so that everyone who has faith in him
may not die but have eternal life.

*Here may follow a seasonal or other special thanksgiving;
or else the prayer continues:*

We thank you that Jesus was born among us;
that he lived our common life on earth;
that he suffered and died for us;
that he rose again;
and that he is always present
through the Holy Spirit.

We thank you that we can live in the faith
that your kingdom will come,
and that in life, in death
and beyond death you are with us.

*Then, or after the special thanksgiving, the prayer
continues:*

Therefore with all the company of heaven,
and with all your people,
of all places and times,
we proclaim your greatness and sing your praise.

All **Holy, holy, holy Lord**
God of power and might,
Heaven and earth are full of your glory.
Hosanna in the highest.

Minister Blessed is he
who comes in the name of the Lord.

All **Hosanna in the highest.**

Minister Holy Lord God,
by what we do here
in remembrance of Christ
we celebrate
his perfect sacrifice on the Cross
and his glorious resurrection and ascension;
we declare
that he is Lord of all;
and we prepare for
his coming in his kingdom.

We pray that
through your Holy Spirit
this bread may be for us
the body of Christ
and this wine
the blood of Christ.

136

Accept our sacrifice of praise;
and as we eat and drink
at his command
unite us to Christ
as one body in him,
and give us strength
to serve you in the world.

And to you,
one holy and eternal God,
Father, Son and Holy Spirit,
we give praise and glory,
now and for ever. **Amen.**

The Lord's Prayer

Minister   And now, as our Saviour Christ
has taught us, we say,

All   **Our Father in heaven,
hallowed be your Name,
your kingdom come,
your will be done,
on earth as in heaven.
Give us today our daily bread.
Forgive us our sins
as we forgive those who sin against us.
Do not bring us to the time of trial
but deliver us from evil.
For the kingdom, the power, and the glory are
      yours
now and for ever.   Amen.**

The Breaking of the Bread   (*all sit*)

Minister   The Lord Jesus
on the night when he was betrayed
took bread (*here the minister takes the
bread in his hands*), and when he had given thanks,
he broke it (*here the minister
breaks the bread*), and said,
'This is my body which is for you.
Do this in remembrance of me.'

In the same way also the cup (*here the minister
raises the cup*), saying,
'This cup is the new convenant in my blood.
Do this, as often as you drink it,
in remembrance of me.'

Or, if the narrative of the institution has been used earlier in the service, as he breaks the bread the minister may say:

The bread which we break
is the communion of the body of Christ.

And as he raises the cup he may say:

The cup of blessing which we bless
is the communion of the blood of Christ.

The Sharing of the Bread and Wine

In giving the bread the minister says:

Take, eat; this is the body of Christ
which is broken for you;
do this in remembrance of him.

or,

The body of our Lord Jesus Christ,
given for you.

In giving the cup the minister says:

This cup is the new covenant
in the blood of Christ,
shed for you and for many
for the remission of sins:
drink of it.

or,

The blood of our Lord Jesus Christ,
shed for you.

Acclamation *(may be said or sung)*

Minister   Let us praise the Lord.
All   **Christ has died.**
           Christ is risen.
           In Christ shall all be made alive.

           Blessing and honour and glory and
           power be to our God for ever and
           ever.   Amen.

Prayer after Communion

Minister   Let us pray.

Most gracious God,
we praise you
for what you have given
and for what you have promised us here.

You have made us one
with all your people
in heaven and on earth.
You have fed us
with the bread of life,
and renewed us for your service.

Now we give ourselves to you;
and we ask
that our daily living
may be part of the life of your kingdom,

and that our love
may be your love reaching out into the life of the
      world;
through Jesus Christ our Lord. **Amen.**

Hymn or Doxology

Dismissal and Blessing

Minister   Go in peace to serve the Lord;
and the blessing of God Almighty,
the Father, the Son and the Holy Spirit,
be with you always. **Amen.**

ALPHABETICAL INDEX OF TUNES

Abel, 2
Abingdon, 56, 57
Ach Gott und Herr, 35
Ackergill, 43
All kinds of light, 22
Askerswell, 74, 91
Au clair de la lune, 45
Ave virgo virginum, 11

Babel, 85
Beatitudes, 86
Birabus, 1 (i)
Blackbird Leys, 97
Bridegroom, 4
Bunessan, 78

Caerlaverock, 48 (ii)
Celebration, 87
Charlestown, 1 (ii)
Chereponi, 44
Cheshunt, 83
Christe Sanctorum, 10
City of God, 58
Come my way, 15 (ii)
Corbridge, 33
Cornwall, 67

Deane, 93 (i)
Dieu nous avons vu, 36
Dollis Brook, 16
Durrow, 18

Edmondsham, 69
Emley Moor, 48 (i)
Engelberg, 106
Every Star, 20

Fifehead, 102
Forgive our sins, 25 (i)
Franconia, 59
Fudgie, 17

Gatescarth, 27
Gaudium et Spes, 99
Genevan Psalm 98, 66
Glencaple, 61

Goffs Oak, 88
Green Lake, 94

Hambleden, 37
Hampton Poyle, 55
Harvest, 71
Hermon, 25 (ii)
Holnicote, 93 (ii)

Ilfracombe, 28
Illsley, 109
Intercessor, 103

John One, 68
Jonathan, 51

King's Langley, 95
Kum ba yah, 49

Lark in the clear air, 105
Laudate pueri, 79
Lauds, 98
Let the cosmos, 50
Litherop, 52
Lord we remember, 62
Lumis, 3

Maiden Way, 7
Malham, 101
Mayfield, 24 (ii)

Naphill, 76

One Fifty, 80 (i)
Orientis Partibus, 80 (ii)
Osborne, 77

Paddock Place, 6
Patterns, 90
Petersfield, 46
Philippian, 104
Pious Prayers, 107
Platts Lane, 5
Polzeath, 12

Quedgeley, 14
Quittez, pasteurs, 72

Rasumovsky, 81
Rawthorpe, 54
Rodel, 8 (i)

St. Bartholomew, 65
St. Bavon, 19
St. Ethelwald, 96
St. Mary's, 9
San Rocco, 60
See the baby, 84
Shaker Tune, 41
Shepherd Boy's Song, 38
Shrub End, 40
Sing Hosanna, 26
Solothurn, 70
Song 20, 64
Stein, 89
Stoner Hill, 63
Sunset, 13
Sussex, 34
Swithen, 108

Te Deum, 21
The Hayes, 24 (i)
Theodoric, 30
Torphins, 8 (ii)
Transfiguration, 75
Trotting, 100
Tunbridge, 15 (i)
Turriff, 31

Ubi Caritas, 29

Wansbeck, 53
Waterloo, 42
Westholme, 23
Winchcombe, 39
Winton, 92
Woodmansterne, 73
Worlebury, 82

Yisu ne Kaha, 47

Zeals, 32

INDEX OF COMPOSERS, ARRANGERS AND SOURCES OF TUNES

A number in italics indicates a Harmonization, Arrangement, or Descai

Ainslie, J., 82
Alden, J. H., 38
American Folk Hymn, 1 (ii)
Andachts Zymbeln (Freiburg, 1655), 35

Bach, J. S., *35*
Bäck, S., 85
Barrett-Ayres, R., 2, 8 (ii)
Bartlett, L. F., 80 (i)
Birch, J., *41*
Bishop, J., 109
Blake, L., 39, 43
Brent Smith, A., 15 (ii)

Carey, H., 77
Carter, S., 20, 41
Clarke, J., 15 (i), 25 (ii)
Cutts, P. W., 1 (i), 4, 24 (ii), 40, 48 (i), 52, 54, 55, 74, 91, 97, 101, 108

Darke, H., 76
Dearnley, C., 75
Duncalf, H., 65
Dykes Bower, J., 14
Dyson, G., 92

English Traditional Melody, 12, 34, 95
Evans, D., *10, 18*

French Melody, 45, 72, 80 (ii)

Gaelic Melody, 78
Gardner, J., 28
Gibbons, O., 64
Goodall, D. S., 42, 107
Gooding, Y., 90
Green, J., 50

Harris, W. H., 46, 63
Havergal, W. H., 59
Holst, G., *30*
Horn, J., *Gesangbuch* (1544), 11
Hutchings, A. J. B., 17

Irish Traditional Melody, 18, 105

Jacquet, R. H., 83, 88

Jagger, A. T. I., 19

Kentucky Melody, 25 (i)
König, *Harmonischer-Liederschat* (1738), 59

Langlais, J., 36
Laycock, G., 71, *84*
Llewellyn, W., 86
Loring, J. H., 69

McCarthy, D., 87
Micklem, T. C., 3, 6, 8 (i), 16, 22, 27, 32, 48 (ii), 61, 68, 73, 93 (i), 102, 104
Moe, D., 58
Murray, A. G., 29
Monk, W. H., 96

Negro Melody, 49, 84
Newport, D., 62
North Ghanaian Melody, 44

Paris Antiphoner (1681), 10
Parry, C. H. H., 103
Piae Cantiones (1582), 30
Potter, D., 9

Reid, E., 23, 31, 100
Routley, E. R., 7, 21, 24 (i), 33, 53, 56, 57, 94, 110, 111, 112
Russian Melody, 81

Schweizer, R., 89
Sharpe, E., 5
Shaw, M., *72, 81*
Sheldon, R., 51
Stanford, C. V., 106
Stanton, W. K., 37
Stocks, G. G., 13

Strange, C. E., 93 (ii)
Strasbourg, La Forme des Prieres (1545), 66
Swann, D., *42*
Swiss Traditional Melody, 70

Thiman, E. H., *80 (ii)*
Traditional Melody, 26

Urdu Melody, 47

Vaughan Williams, R., *34, 77, 95*

Wesley, S. S., 67
Westbrook, F., *47*
Williams, D., 60
Wilson, J., *65, 80 (i)*, 98
Wren, B. A., 99

Young, C. R., *1 (ii)*

Zimmermann, H. W., 79

INDEX OF AUTHORS, TRANSLATORS AND SOURCES OF WORDS

A number in italics indicates a Translation

Appleford, P., 46
Arlott, J., 34

Bayly, A. F., 48, 60, 78, 109
Bevan, E. F., *4*
Bonhoeffer, D., 63
Bridge, B. E., 96
Bridges, R., 64
Bunyan, J., 38
Burkitt, F. C., 76

Caird, G. B., 67
Carter, S., 20, 41
Collihole, M., 83
Cropper, M., 45, 95

Dearmer, P., 30, 72, *81*
Dudley-Smith T., 92
Dunn V., 50

Farquharson, W. H. *63*
Ferguson, J., 2
Fraser, I. M., 8, 54

Gaunt, A., 13, 56
Gaunt, H. C. A., 14, 73
Geyer, J. B., 23
Gill, D. M., 12
Goodall, D. S., 42, 108
Green, F. Pratt, 10, 28, 51, 59, 87, *89*, 94, 106
Gregory, J. K., 19, 37, 107

Hartman, O. 85
Herbert, G., 15
Herklots, R. E., 25
Herve, M. O., 88
Hewlett, M., 75
Hilton, D., 90
Hughes, D. W., 7, 17

Icarus, P., 82, 97

Jillson, M., 79
Johnson, R., *36*
Jones, R. G., 32

Kaan, F., 5, 33, 53, 70, 71, 77, 80, 91, 103
King G., 105

Liturgy of Malabar, 29
Luff, A., *21*

Micklem, T. C., 3, 6, 16, 22, 27, 69, 101, 104
Micklem, R. & T. C., *85*
Monahan, D., *47*

New English Bible, 68
North Ghanaian Hymn, 44

O'Neill, J., 62
Orchard, S., 61

Phillips, A., 43
Pilcher, C. V., 35

Quinn, J., *29*

Reid, E., 31, 100
Rimaud, D., 36
Routley, E. R., 1, *66*

Stein, P., 89

Tauler, J., *4*
Thompson, C., 11
Traditional, 26, 49, 84

Watts, I., 64, 65
Wren, B. A., 9, 18, 24, *36*, 39, 40, 52, 55, 57, 58, 74, 93, 98, 99, 102

INDEX OF FIRST LINES

All who love and serve your city 1
Although we cannot see, we believe 3
"Am I my brother's keeper?" 2
As the bridegroom to his chosen 4
As we break the bread 5
Awake from sleep, the night is spent 6
Beyond the mist and doubt 7
Christ, burning past all suns 8
Christ is alive! Let Christians sing 9
Christ is the world's Light, he and none other 10
Christian people, raise your song 11
Come let us remember the joys of the town 12
Come, living God, when least expected 13
Come, Lord, to our souls come down 14
Come, my way, my truth, my life 15
Come to our homes to stay 16
Creator of the earth and skies 17
Deep in the shadows of the past 18
Early morning. "Come, prepare him" 19
Every star shall sing a carol 20
Extol the Lord your God 21
Father, we thank you 22
Fire is lighting torch and lamp at night 23
For the bread that we have eaten 24
"Forgive our sins as we forgive" 25
Give me joy in my heart, keep me praising 26
Give to me, Lord, a thankful heart 27
Glorious the day when Christ was born 28
God is love, and where true love is 29
God is love: his the care 30
God is our friend, Jesus is our friend 31
God of concrete, God of steel 32
God who spoke in the beginning 33
God, whose farm is all creation 34
God, your glory we have seen in your Son 36
Good is our God who made this place 37
He that is down needs fear no fall 38
Here hangs a man discarded 40
Here, Lord, we take the broken bread 35
I come with joy to meet my Lord 39
I danced in the morning 41
I want to go out 42
Into a world of dark 43
Jesu, Jesu, fill us with your love 44
Jesus' hands were kind hands 45

Jesus, humble was your birth 46
Jesus the Lord says, I am the Bread 47
Joy wings to God our song 48
Kum ba yah, my Lord 49
Let the cosmos ring 50
Life has many rhythms 51
Life is great! So sing about it 52
Lord, as we rise to leave this shell of worship 53
Lord, bring the day to pass 54
Lord Christ, the Father's mighty Son 55
Lord Christ, we praise your sacrifice 56
Lord God, your love has called us here 57
Lord Jesus, if I love and serve my neighbour 58
Lord Jesus, once a child 59
Lord of the boundless curves of space 60
Lord, we remember your people 62
Lord, you give to us the precious gift of life 61
Men go to God when they are sorely placed 63
My God, my king, thy various praise 65
My Lord, my Life, my Love 64
New songs of celebration render 66
No one has ever seen God 68
Not far beyond the sea, nor high 67
Nothing in all creation 69
Now join we, to praise the creator 71
Now let us from this table rise 70
Now quit your care, your anxious fear and worry 72
O God, by whose almighty plan 73
Once from a European shore 74
Once on a mountain top there stood three startled men 75
Our Lord, his passion ended 76
Out of our failure to create 77
Praise and thanksgiving 78
Praise the Lord! Praise, you servants of the Lord 79
Praise the Lord with joyful cry 80
Praise to God in the highest 81
Reap me the earth as a harvest to God 82
Ring a bell for peace 83
See the baby lying in a manger 84
See them building Babel's tower 85
Show us your ways, O Lord 86
Sing, one and all, a song of celebration 87
Sing to the Lord, stars and beautiful sun 88
Sing to the Lord a new song 89
Skipping down the pavement wide 90
Surrounded by a world of need 91
Tell out, my soul, the greatness of the Lord 92
Thank you, Lord, for water, soil and air 93
The Church of Christ, in every age 94
The glory of our King was seen 95
The Son of God proclaim 96
The voice of God goes out to all the world 97

There's a spirit in the air 98
This we can do for justice and for peace 99
Trotting, trotting through Jerusalem 100
Under the arches of the night 101
We are your people 102
We praise you, Lord, for all that's true and pure 104
We turn to you, O God of every nation 103
When I see the salmon leap the fall 105
When in man's music, God is glorified 106
When you started off the universe 107
Where is God today ? 108
Your light, O God, was given to man 109